WHEN YOU'RE A JET

WHEN YOU'RE A JET

The Story of A Dancer's Extraordinary, Ordinary Life

David Bean

The Attic Studio
PUBLISHING HOUSE
Clinton Corners, NY

WHEN YOU'RE A JET
The Story of a Dancer's Extraordinary, Ordinary Life
by David Bean

All cover and endsheet images are from the MGM archives for the 1961 movie, West Side Story: *David Bean (front cover); poster (front cover and interior pages); Jets singing the "Jet Song" (back cover; see list of names on page 98); Front endsheet (David "Tiger" Bean is on the far right); Back endsheet (see list of dancers and full image on pages 100-101).* West Side Story © 1961 Metro-Goldwyn-Mayer Studios Inc. All Rights Reserved. Courtesy of MGM Media Licensing.

Illustration Credits: see pages 229-233 — including copyrights, credits, and comments.

THE ATTIC STUDIO Publishing House • PO Box 75 • Clinton Corners, NY 12514

To contact the publisher, please email: atticstudiopress@aol.com

To contact the author, please email: westsidetiger61@gmail.com

PRINTED IN THE UNITED STATES OF AMERICA

Library of Congress Cataloging-in-Publication Data

Names: Bean, David, 1939– author.

Title: When you're a Jet : the story of a dancer's extraordinary, ordinary life / David Bean.

Description: Clinton Corners : The Attic Studio Publishing House, 2021. |

Includes index. |

Summary: "*When You're A Jet* offers a richly illustrated account of the extraordinary, ordinary life of David Bean, a dancer, husband, father, and entrepreneur. From tap dancing on the streets of Hollywood, to Broadway performances as a young teenager, David grew up in the world of theatre. He appeared in *Peter Pan* on Broadway with Mary Martin and Cyril Ritchard. He danced in the stage production of *West Side Story* and then performed as Tiger in the 1961 film version starring Natalie Wood. The book ends when, six decades later, Steven Spielberg taps David for a cameo in the remake of *West Side Story*. David and his wife Jean, also a dancer, performed over the years in theatre and television shows together. They also built a network of businesses with the passion of a couple on a mission. Hobnobbing with celebrities in New York, London and Hollywood, they were comfortable building every passion into a business. Their success was pure theatre. David lives with his wife of sixty years in upstate New York. His daughter Jennifer is married to James, a New York City fireman, and they have four children, Bryce, Connor, and twins Jake and Madison." — Provided by publisher.

Identifiers: LCCN 2021032984 | ISBN 9781883551216 (hardcover)

Subjects: LCSH: Bean, David, 1939– | Dancers — United States — Biography

Classification: LCC GV1785.B34975 A3 2021 | DDC 792.802/8092 [B] — dc22

LC record available at https://lccn.loc.gov/2021032984

For Jeanie & Jennifer

I gratefully and lovingly dedicate this book
to my wife Jean and our daughter Jennifer
and her family — all of whom have been so
vital in putting the extraordinary in my life.

David Bean in West Side Story
London Production, 1958

CONTENTS

Foreword

by Michael Korda

F. SCOTT FITZGERALD wrote that "there are no second acts in American lives," but he was wrong. David Bean's life proves, on the contrary, that there are indeed second acts, third acts, epilogues and even revivals. He has been a child star, a hugely successful dancer and actor on Broadway and in London and on film. He has also been, with his beloved wife Jeanie, a successful restaurateur in Clinton Corners, NY.

Now in his 80s, David Bean has even reprised his appearance in *West Side Story*, albeit in a different role — and that is not even to mention that he is a passionate aviator, a devoted family man, and an inspired raconteur.

His book takes him from his debut as a child star (in *Peter Pan*, starring Mary Martin) through a long and star-studded theatrical career, and to a glittering cast of friends and film and theatre "greats."

When You're A Jet is not only a joy to read, but it communicates to the reader throughout his own *joie de vivre,* his passionate enthusiasm for the theatre and for life, and the intense love that has kept Jeanie and him married, as partners, lovers and mutual admirers for nearly sixty years — "a class act" if ever there was one. For anyone who loves the theatre, his book is a "must read," as brilliant, witty and lively as his own remarkable career.

Prolific writer Michael Korda, former editor-in-chief of Simon and Schuster, is the author of more than thirty books, including Charmed Lives, Hero, Country Matters, *and* With Wings Like Eagles.

Prologue

What A Difference A Day Makes

THE TELEPHONE RANG. It was a call from Nick Petrovich, an associate with the Cindy Tolan Casting Agency in New York City. Would I be available on July 14, 2019, for a walk-on role or even a possible part in Steven Spielberg's remake of *West Side Story*, shooting on 128th Street in Harlem?

"There are two roles available," Nick explained. "You might play one of the cops, or you might be the shop owner who sells fabric to Anita at the beginning of the musical number *America*."

"Well," I said, "perhaps you'd like me to do a short screen test? I've been out of the business for almost 40 years. I'm sure your casting director has no idea who I am, or what I'm capable of doing. She probably wasn't even born then."

Nick laughed.

"Are you kidding, Mr. Bean? I don't think there's a single person on this production who doesn't know you. You and the other dancers from the original *West Side Story* are legends."

Offering such encouraging words, he continued.

"The wardrobe department from Steiner Studios in Brooklyn will contact you and you'll have a fitting on Saturday the 13th. Corey Sklov, from the production office, will call you and arrange hotel accommodations and there will be a van to pick you up at your hotel for your ride to Harlem."

Nearly sixty years after filming the original *West Side Story,* I was about to make my "comeback" in Steven Spielberg's new production of the movie. *Wow!*

~ 1 ~

Growing Up a Bean

I WAS BORN on December 4, 1939, at the General Hospital in Los Angeles (now the University of Southern California Medical Center). I am the youngest of six children, making me the baby of the family, a position I have relished all these years. With screaming red hair and large freckles that tried to hide my dimples, I was spoiled with love from everyone.

I was three years old when my brother Don had to be taken to the General Hospital for a check-up. Undoubtedly the only reason I was in tow to the hospital was that we couldn't afford a babysitter.

As my mother recounts the story, while Don was being checked by the physician, I had a seizure right there in my mother's arms. Clearly, I was in the right place at the right time (a line that follows me throughout my life). In the early '40s, there was a polio epidemic in Los Angeles, and I had become part of the epidemic. I have no idea how long I remained in the hospital. The Sister Kenny treatment was in effect for polio victims, and Mother was given instructions on how to treat me, which included hot packs and exercise.

As the polio epidemic filled the beds in the hospital, I was released into my family's care using that Sister Kenny treatment. Don, Doug, and Jerry were old enough to help Mother keep hot packs on my entire body 24/7. Within a few months, I had completely recovered and have suffered no ill effects.

My growth spurt didn't happen until I was fifteen, and I'm sure Mother started my dance lessons to build strength in my small eight-year-old body. To pay for lessons, Mother played piano for the dance school and I took tap dancing. I was not allowed to take ballet. "That's for girls," my stepdad, "Beanie" would say. "Boys mow the lawn, work outside and tap dance. Girls clean house, cook and take ballet!" And so it was…I took tap. I loved tap and never had to be reminded to practice.

As far as I knew, my childhood was outstanding. And I was the happiest kid on the planet. In my mind, nothing seemed to be less than perfect; but in reality life was a bit more complicated than that.

We lived in a "great house"— two bedrooms, one bath, and eight people. *What?* A family of eight in a two-bedroom house? Well, it happened, and I never gave it a second thought. The four boys in one room, my two sisters in the second bedroom, and my parents sleeping in the living room on a sofa bed.

There were no doors inside our house. At the end of the hall, three curtains replaced the bedroom and bathroom doors. Privacy didn't exist; but for me, the youngest in the family, I didn't know anything different.

We had a picnic table in the kitchen that seated six of us kids. There was little room for Mom and Dad, who always ate after us. Rarely did any of us stay in the house after a meal. We'd be out until it got dark playing games, like Hide-and-Seek and Kick the Can — or simply hanging out with all the kids in the neighborhood at an open bonfire in our backyard.

No one on our road had a TV. We would all pile into Dad's truck and drive two miles to our friend's home to watch the *Friday Night Fights*. On weekends we couldn't wait to turn on the radio to catch the broadcast of *Let's Pretend, Gangbusters* or *The Green Hornet*. We had a very tall windup Victrola that played 78 vinyl records. *The Bluebird of Happiness* was my favorite recording.

We all wore clothes from out of my dad's tarp tent in the backyard. Dad was a "junk man." Whatever items he collected were put up for sale in the tent. He dealt with scrap metal, auto parts — just about anything saleable, including clothing.

Each year, just before school, I did get a brand new pair of Levis. Other than that, I never had anything new to wear that I can remember. Any extras in our lives had to be earned. Going to the movies at the Tumbleweed Movie House was nine cents for a double feature. Milk Duds were a nickel. Mowing a neighbor's lawn and pulling a few weeds, and *bingo,* I could earn 25 cents. That's a double feature, **two** boxes of Milk Duds, with change coming. I was a happy camper!

"The 180 Rule"

A S A YOUNG BOY, whenever Dad would offer me an important job, I would eagerly accept — not for money (there wasn't any), but for the chance for me to please him.

Before he would tell me what the job was, Dad would typically remind me, "Now this job is really important and I know you'll give me 100%."

"Sure Dad! You give me the job and I'll give you 125%. What's the job?"

As he was loading scrap metal onto the old International truck, I would follow him around.

"What's the job?"

He paused, taking his time to ponder my 125% offer.

"That's what I wanted to hear, Dave. But you know, this job is really important, and I just may need 150%."

"Dad, Dad!" By this time, I would be yelling, as I continued to follow him around the truck. "I'll give you 180%!"

8-year-old David

I'd get the job for sure — as Dad, with a noticeable grin on his face, would continue loading the truck.

As the years went along, the "180 Rule" became a habit. To this day, my wife Jean and I credit our "extraordinary, ordinary life" in good measure to living out the 180 Rule.

SATURDAY NIGHTS

WE LIVED on a small road with five houses. The place to be on a Saturday night was our living room at 1620 Cogswell Road.

Each week, our upright piano got quite a workout as the whole family entertained each other without reserve. During the '40s and early '50s, entertainment by the entire family and neighbors was the norm.

Dad was the starter. Once he stood up and sang the *Jelly Bean Song (a.k.a. He's a Curbstone Cutie),* we all followed … as we heard:

> *Well I'm a curbstone cutie*
> *My Mama's pride and beauty,*
> *They call me Jelly Bean.*
>
> *I part my hair in the middle*
> *Press it down.*
> *I scatter little Jelly Beans*
> *All around town.*
>
> *Oh well, the girls all love me*
> *They think I'm a riot*
> *If you know what I mean.*
>
> *… They call me Jelly Bean.*

16

Dad did the same movements in his song every time. For "I part my hair in the middle," he would put both hands on his head as if to part his hair. Coupling both hands at his waist, he would rock back and forth slowly as he sang. It was a gentle, wonderful song and we all loved it.

Next, Mother would play *Kitten on the Keys* or *Clair de Lune*. Donald would play the trombone. Jerry joined in on the French horn, and my oldest sister Roberta would play the violin.

My other sister Janet and I danced as a team with numbers like *Aba Daba Honeymoon* and *Simple Melody*.

Now Doug, second to the eldest, was incredibly shy. In fact, shy would be an understatement. He didn't play an instrument and didn't dance; but if you cut a hole in a large brown paper bag where his mouth would be and then placed it over his head, he would sing for you — usually a rendition of the nursery rhyme, *"Hey Diddle Diddle, the Cat and the Fiddle, The Cow Jumped over the Moon."* As long as he didn't have to look at anyone, Doug was in fine voice.

Those Saturday evenings were filled with popular songs and show tunes—and lots of laughter. Mom and Dad would play duets

Dad (Beanie) and Mom (Merle)

on the upright like *Beer Barrel Polka* and *Muskrat Ramble*. At times, we had quite an abundance of neighbors in our living room and the singing was grand. Grand enough to call ourselves "The Cogswell Chorus."

DANCE TEACHERS

Melvin Kaiser

MELVIN KAISER was my first professional dance teacher. Tall and thin with golden blond hair, he was full of energy, which made it easy to work hard for him. Mother played the piano for Melvin's school, and after a couple of years, my sister Janet and I became a team there. With musical numbers like *How Could You Believe Me When I Said I Loved You When You Know I've Been a Liar All My Life,* we were a hit!

Melvin had all of his pupils "dancing out" at least once a week at fairs, hospitals, and churches. *Anywhere!* The Norwalk Hospital in California's Orange County was a favorite. Janet and I performed *How Could You Believe Me* at the hospital and they wouldn't let us off the stage.

One of our most memorable gigs was on Hollywood Boulevard. After World War II, not all the shops on the Boulevard were occupied by retailers. One empty space was given to the United Service Organizations (USO) for military servicemen, for whom we danced on the weekends. The best part of our USO gig was the free doughnuts. All you could eat. *Payday!*

At the Pomona State Fair, we were given a truck bed to dance on, equipped with an upright piano at one end. One day, Mother was seated

Dancing siblings: Janet and David

at the piano and it was my turn to dance. I rushed over to her in a panic, saying, "Mom, I can't remember the dance." I had simply drawn a blank!

"Just do wings," Mother replied, not really knowing what other advice to give. Well, that's just what I did. Mother started *I Got Rhythm* and I stayed with the fast and flashy "wings," complete with circular arm movements that were exhausting. The audience started to applaud right away and by the end of the number, we were all exhausted! Three minutes of wings and three minutes of applause.

Melvin was responsible for moving me up to a new teacher in North Hollywood. Out of the blue, he had told Mother that he had taught me everything that he could; soon enough, I moved on to an advanced teacher, Mr. Eddie Gay, when I was twelve.

Eddie Gay

ESCRIBED AS A "teacher to the stars," Eddie Gay taught film stars Vera Ellen *(White Christmas)* and Donald O'Connor *(Singing in the Rain),* as well as the tap dancing Blackburn Twins, who were only seven when they danced in the Jerome Kern musical, *Music in the Air* (1932-33). Richard Beymer, who ended up playing *Tony* in the movie *West Side Story*, was in my class.

From 1952 to 1954, Mother drove me the one-hour trek from El Monte to North Hollywood three times a week. Eddie Gay called me "Champion." It really made me feel special. Later, when I realized he called all of his students "Champion," it didn't diminish the title. I was proud to be his "Champion." In my mind, Eddie Gay was nine feet tall. He wore black stovepipe pants with suspenders (braces). When he moved, his shoulders were like glass; he glided across the floor effortlessly. I tried so hard to be like him.

It was Eddie Gay who changed my life. While Melvin Kaiser sent me out on hundreds of dance exhibitions, Eddie Gay sent me just once. Not to entertain, but to audition.

*Tony Award winners for their roles in
Peter Pan: Mary Martin ("Peter")
and Cyril Ritchard ("Captain Hook")*

~ 2 ~

Peter Pan

THE AUDITION

ON A WARM SUMMER AFTERNOON in 1954, Eddie Gay arranged for most of his students to attend an audition in the enormous hall of the Musician's Union in Hollywood. Because Mother was busy playing the piano at the Del Mar Hotel near San Diego, Dad drove me. It was to be my very first audition — and I had no idea what an "audition" was. It didn't matter. It couldn't be much different from jumping off the back of Dad's truck and tap dancing for people on the sidewalk. I arrived fearless.

Good grief, there were 300 kids there. The floors of the Musician's Union had just been polished and we were not allowed to put on our tap shoes.

Robert Tucker, assistant to the choreographer, gave us dance combinations that were combining jazz and ballet. I could see my dad in the rear of the room, watching me in my stocking feet do this jazz-ballet. *What on earth must he be thinking?* Here I was, doing ballet in front of him, as his firm words were echoing in my mind, "Girls take ballet, boys take tap!"

Another man, the choreographer Jerome Robbins, would stop us, correct us, and have us do it once again. While walking back and forth as he watched us, he would laugh. We must have been a sight doing ballet in our stocking feet. I'll never forget his laugh. It was a giggle, full of happy sounds that seemed to give me confidence.

Later he asked what I was prepared to sing.

"Well, sir," I replied, "I haven't prepared anything, but I can sing anything you like! How about *Yankee Doodle*?"

He said, "Sure," and after I belted it out, another hundred kids sang *Yankee Doodle.*

The audition lasted three days and each new day there were another hundred kids. For the recall on the third day, my Mother drove me, bringing along my two older sisters, Roberta and Janet, just to watch. While I was waiting to be called, I heard a "stage mother" say to her son, "Now sparkle, Freddie!" It was her way of cheering him on as his name was called. To this day, whenever someone in our family needs a lift, we sing out, "Sparkle, Freddie!"

The first day of auditioning came to an end, and I was asked to return the following day. As it turned out, the audition was for the show *Peter Pan,* James M. Barrie's iconic tale of a "Lost Boy's" adventures in "Never-Never Land." Mary Martin would play *Peter Pan* and Cyril Ritchard would play the villainous *Captain Hook.* The show would be directed and choreographed by Jerome Robbins. Ultimately, the show would be heading to Broadway. Imagine that: auditioning for a Broadway show in California! Who would have thought? Another instance of being in the right place at the right time.

By the third day, I had a positive feeling that I would be awarded a part. Before the end of the day, they had lined up all seven Lost Boys in a row. And I was among them.

The Lost Boy I became was "Slightly Soiled," a nugget of a character created by the author. In Barrie's classic tale, if you're lost at birth for more than seven days, you're sent to Never-Never Land. If you arrive there with no name, Peter must name you. *Aha,* there's the catch. As a Lost Boy, my mother had written "Slightly Soiled" on the shirt I wore when I was lost. So, that's my name — the only Lost Boy who came with a name.

Rehearsals

Soon after all the "Lost Boys" went through the red tape of joining Actors Equity and getting a physical, rehearsals started in Los Angeles.

Getting into the union was difficult. If you didn't belong to the union, you didn't get hired. But you couldn't belong to the union unless you'd been hired. A real *Catch-22.* In our case, the Los Angeles Civic Light Opera, and Edwin Lester, producer of the show, came to our rescue and sponsored us.

Rehearsals were at the Musician's Union, where the auditions had been held. There was a massive room ("The Hall") with a stage at the far end. The seats for the audience had been removed, and we worked in the flat area on a tiled floor. It was not a theatre — more like a meeting hall with a stage. The dancers had it rough, as the tiled floor had no give, and Jerome Robbins worked these young performers extremely hard.

It was the summer of 1954 and blistering hot in Los Angeles. Not an ideal time to be working as a dancer for Jerome Robbins, a choreographer with a reputation for being brutal. He *was* brutal, having them repeat the dances over and over again. "OK, once more...from the top!"

At the end of the day, their poor feet were bleeding and they were exhausted. It never occurred to me that one day I would be one of those dancers, ultimately going through the same brutal rehearsals for the same man in *West Side Story.* For now, I was a fourteen-year-old "Lost Boy" having the time of my life.

Staging the song *I Won't Grow Up* with Mary Martin was easy and so much fun. Near the end of the song I had a solo where I stood up and sang, "I won't grow up! No I promise that I won't...I will stay a boy forever...and be banished if I don't."

Jerome Robbins asked me to growl the "I," so I growled it out, *"I–I–I–I–I–I–I–I won't grow up"!* He loved it. ...And there came that laugh again. Every time you heard that giggle–laugh of his, you knew you were on the right track.

Cyril Ritchard played the inimitable "Captain Hook" who terrified no one, frightened few, and was secretly loved by everyone. His soliloquy "No little children love me," was far from true. All little children, young and old, loved him.

Cyril's wife Madge was with him during the rehearsals in LA and San Francisco. She hung out with Margalo Gillmore, the English-born American actress who played Mrs. Darling in *Peter Pan.*

The adults loved having the Lost Boys around as we entertained them. We would make up song and dance numbers (tap of course), performing them during our breaks. There was always an upright piano handy, and I played all the songs my mother had taught me. Cyril encouraged me to play on our breaks. My songs made them laugh. I had signed a "run of the show" contract. And I was actually getting paid for all this fun!

We traveled to San Francisco, opening at the Curran Theatre. Rehearsals were on stage or in the foyer. One morning, Cyril Ritchard and the Pirates were using the stage and we were in the foyer with Mary Martin rehearsing *I Won't Grow Up.*

Mary decided to take a break. She hopped up on the piano and sang just for us kids, *My Heart Belongs to Daddy,* the Cole Porter song she made famous in the musical *Leave It To Me.* Moments like that live forever.

Arriving in Los Angeles to open at the Philharmonic, management decided that an extra musical number was needed. As the second act opens, Wendy flies into Never-Never Land; we (the Lost Boys) think she is a "Windy Bird" and we shoot her with an arrow. Luckily, the arrow hits a locket she is wearing and she is unharmed. However, Peter is upset and doesn't want to move her, so he comes up with a plan to build a house around her.

This being the premise, Jule Styne, Betty Comden and Adolph Green were brought in to write an additional song to fit the occasion of building a house for Wendy! In an empty rehearsal hall, Jule Styne filled us in on what the three of them had been working on.

"This is what we've come up with," Jule said to us, and proceeded to sing, *"Let's be quiet as a mouse and build a lovely little house for Wendy, so that Wendy, she's here to stay, and be our mother, at last we have a mother."* He sang the entire song and then, turning to the Lost Boys who were sitting on the floor in rapt attention, he explained that Peter was to sing the song and we would all join in singing in harmony.

"We need to know what key you sing in!," he exclaimed.

Looking straight at me, he said, "David, what key do you sing in?"

"Well, Mr. Styne, I don't know what key I sing in, but if you get up from that piano I'll sing a song for you and maybe you can tell me what key I'm singing in!"

With that, I sat at the piano and sang, *My Cutey's Due at Two-To-Two Today.* A wonderful old ditty mother taught me that rambles on for at least four minutes. By the end of it, Jule was on the floor in stitches, and from behind the piano I heard Adolph Green say, "You sang that in the key of F!" Another fun moment to remember.

While *Peter Pan* was playing in Los Angeles, Mother brought her mother, Gramma Richey, to the Philharmonic to see the show.

Gramma was in her 80s, and on the drive home we were all excited to hear what she thought about the show.

"What did you think of Mary Martin?" Mother asked.

"Well, she was just wonderful," adding with much more enthusiasm, "And what about the little boy in the green suit? Wasn't he wonderful, too?"

Mary Martin, "the little boy in the green suit"

ON OUR WAY TO BROADWAY

WITH SAN FRANCISCO AND LOS ANGELES BEHIND US, we were off to New York City. We didn't just *go* there; the company booked an entire train — the Southern Pacific Railroad — with beautiful old Pullman cars, private rooms and tablecloths in the dining car. Three days and three nights — what a great way to see our country!

Cyril Ritchard had a 1941 Chrysler and needed to hire someone to drive it back to New York. While we all took the train, Beanie and his dad, Grampa Leo, both drove Cyril's car cross-country.

Working together on *Peter Pan* was fast becoming a family affair. Dad was hoping for a job driving a truck once we arrived in New York. As it turned out, the truckers were on strike, so he was unemployed. I mentioned it to Cyril during a rehearsal. And, it just so happened that his personal dresser (known as a "gentleman's gentleman") who had assisted him with costume changes backstage, was leaving and needed to be replaced.

The next thing I knew, Dad was on the scene, dressing "Captain Hook." Here's a man who most likely never washed a pair of his own socks in his life, and now he's styling Cyril's wigs and actually dressing someone. He had changed overnight. *Big time!* And it was now permissible for me to take ballet. (Jerome Robbins was happy about that.) Dad started cooking; he even took up oil painting. The transformation was like some Disney movies: unbelievable and a little scary, but most of all, unbelievable.

Rehearsals began in a studio on 54th and Eighth Avenue. One day, Mary Martin noticed that my very red hair was growing out of control, so she decided to give this Lost Boy a needed trim. Walking down the hall, we ran into Perry Como. The popular crooner was rehearsing for a TV special. Mary mentioned that we were looking for an empty room to cut my hair.

"I'm a barber you know," he said. "Singing is just my hobby. You'll need some help." They both cut my hair. *I didn't even leave a tip.*

CURTAIN UP

THE LOST BOYS shared a dressing room in the theatre. Our schedule called for us to arrive an hour before curtain, giving us enough time to take care of makeup and get into costume. It was a thrilling atmosphere. But because we didn't appear in the show until the second act, we had a lot of time to kill. It didn't take long before we had jigsaw puzzles and paint boards filling every available space in the dressing room. A speaker hung on the wall that piped in the activity from on stage.

Opening night of *Peter Pan* on Broadway, October 21, 1954, was special and eventful. During the song *I Won't Grow Up,* my costume didn't hold up. I was wearing a pony-skin vest and a pair of canvas pants. As I stood on cue to sing *I Won't Grow Up* in the growling voice, my pants split! I tried to cover it with my left hand while motioning the lyric with my right, but it didn't work. Because the audience was in on the mishap, it simply became part of the song, just that once.

In Act II, the Pirates capture all of the Lost Boys and keep them prisoners on the ship. As we would huddle together down stage left, *Captain Hook* would roar, "Now then, me buckaroos, I've room on the ship for two cabin boys. Which of ya is it to be?" But on different nights, ol' *Captain Hook* would change the dialog. Instead of calling us "buckaroos," he would call us "turkeys" or "chickadees." The deal was that if he made us laugh, we owed him fifty cents. On the other hand, if we broke him up, he owed us fifty cents.

The first time he called us "turkeys" was on Thanksgiving Day. The audience was in on the joke so his ad-lib was permissible. He continued, "I'd have you all out for dinner, but we are out of cranberries."

Our response was to reply to the cabin boy question as each of us stood and said the same thing rapidly, "I don't think my mother would like me to be a cabin boy. Would your mother like you to be a cabin boy, Toodles?" "I don't think my mother would like me to be a cabin boy. Would your mother like you to be a cabin boy, Slightly?" At that point, I would repeat the sentence and hand it off to the next Lost Boy.

One evening, *Captain Hook* called us "pipsqueaks." I stood when asked the question and said, "I don't think my mother would like me to be a cabin boy or a pipsqueak!"

Taking everyone by surprise, the Lost Boys burst out laughing and Hook fell off his stool. But I didn't even crack a smile, standing there biting my lip.

Counting all the boys and Hook at fifty cents each, that was $4.50 in my pocket. Management never said a word to me, but everyone else got a lecture about professionalism. And *Captain Hook* was asked to keep his ad-libs on the down low, which he found impossible to do.

The cast members of *Peter Pan* soon became one large family. The dancers were extraordinary, working and surviving the ever watchful eye of Jerome Robbins. He was a taskmaster for sure. If you did what he asked of you, no problem. But offering a lame excuse for a lackadaisical

"Curtain Up at Sardi's," 1954

ORKING ON BROADWAY has its perks, even at a young age. During the run of *Peter Pan*, Mary Martin's daughter, Heller Halliday, celebrated her thirteenth birthday. The kids in the show were invited to a party at Sardi's — our first experience at the famed theatre restaurant. In this photo, Heller is at the head of the table, and I'm to her immediate left. *(See list of guests on p. 230.)*

performance was never tolerated. If Jerry didn't get 100%, he became intolerant and sometimes downright nasty.

My only negative experience with Jerry came during the dress rehearsal in Los Angeles. The cast of *The King and I* was invited to our dress rehearsal. In the second act, the Lost Boys open with a lot of banter and I messed up on a line and gave a grimace onstage, way out of character.

After the scene, Jerry stormed up to me and verbally laid me out. "Never make a face if you miss a line. You are professional and I will throw you out of the theatre if I see you do that again. My God, you were acting like a child!" (News flash: I *was* a child.)

Jerry stormed away as fiercely as he had arrived. But he never ever said a harsh word to me again, ever. And, for the next eight years, I gave him not 100% but 180%.

At the end of every show, Mary would step out at the curtain calls and talk to the audience while the cast stood behind her. She thanked the audience and told them a tidbit or two and completely won over their hearts. She was amazing. On one particular night, she mentioned that a very special guest was in the audience who had agreed to come on stage and say hello to everyone.

"Ladies and Gentlemen, Noel Coward."

As he was walking out on stage, Mary turned to me and motioned with her finger for me to stand by her. I walked out and stood to her left, with Mr. Coward on her right.

"Mr. Noel Coward" she said, "This is David Bean."

She looked at me and said, "David Bean, this is Noel Coward"! There was a theatrical pause, and she continued.

"Now I'll let you all in on a little secret. Noel Coward's very first professional role was "Slightly Soiled" in *Peter Pan*.

It really must have been great fun being a part of Mary's audience. She was so genuine and exciting. She made you feel as though she were there just for you and you alone. Audiences adored her.

MARY MARTIN

EVERYONE LOVED MARY. This woman was huggable. Mary's career was established early, not in the theatre but in the Hollywood film industry. In fact, before her theatre career blossomed, Mary had well over a dozen films to her credit.

One story she was fond of telling had to do with Richard Rodgers and Oscar Hammerstein writing a musical titled *Green Grow the Lilacs*. They had offered the lead to Mary while at the same time she was offered *Dancing in the Streets*. What to do?

While having lunch with her husband Richard Halliday at the famed Brown Derby in Hollywood, Mary took a call from Oscar, inquiring if she had made a decision to accept their offer to star in *Green Grow the Lilacs*. During the phone call, she asked her husband for a quarter and she proceeded to

Mary Martin and I during a recording session of "I Won't Grow Up" for the **Peter Pan** *album*

flip it, heads for *Lilacs* and tails for *Dancing in the Streets*. The quarter flip-flopped and settled tails up. *Dancing* closed in Boston never to open again. *Lilacs* underwent a name change and the smash hit musical *Oklahoma* became history.

Cyril Ritchard and Mary had the identical birthday: December 1st. During the entire 23 years I knew Cyril, he and Mary rarely missed contacting each other at least once a year, often on their shared birthday.

CYRIL RITCHARD

CAPTAIN HOOK *(a.k.a. Cyril Ritchard)* was larger than life on stage and off. He was a towering man, well over six feet tall, with an English deportment that made him stand out in the crowd. We were always welcome in his dressing room during the Broadway run. Madge Elliott, the Captain's wife, would frequently ask me back to their apartment between shows for dinner on matinee days. At the time, I was 14 years old and not aware they had lost a son who would have been my age.

After the Broadway run of *Peter Pan*, I split my time between school and traveling from Los Angeles to New York, auditioning for shows and commercials. When in New York, I stayed with Cyril and Madge. I was a tagalong with "The Boss" (one of several nicknames for him). When he would be invited out to dinner parties, shows, or even his show rehearsals,

Cyril is still widely remembered today for his acclaimed performances on stage and screen as **Captain Hook.**

I went along with him. I was a fly on the wall witnessing the celebrity life.

When writing letters or leaving Cyril notes, I affectionately called him *Cyrrrrrrrr.* Madge called him 'Cede Darling.' In turn, Cyril called me by several nicknames: "The Horse" (a favorite), "The Beast," or "Dear Boy" — whichever one found me in his respective favor at the time.

Born in 1898 in Sydney, Australia, his full given name was Cyril Joseph Trimnell-Ritchard. Since his surname was much too long for any theatre marquee, Cyril cut it down to simply "Ritchard," giving the first part, "Trimnell," to his dog. Born into wealth, he was quick to adopt the motto, *Optimum Semper,* only the best. Fond of telling stories of his childhood, Cyril once recounted a visit to his family's haberdasher, where they inquired of the young boy, "And how can we fit you today, Master Ritchard?"

"Only the best, only the best," he recalled saying as a ten year old, fostering the development of what would become his adult stature and deportment.

MADGE ELLIOTT

G LYCERIN AND ROSEWATER, *pale soft skin, pink cheeks, and a deportment of English royalty.* These are the thoughts that glide through my head at the mention of Madge (Leah Madeleine Elliott), the wife of Cyril Ritchard.

Contrary to her grand reputation, I found Madge (a.k.a. "Maddie") to be quiet, reserved and absolutely charming. I first met her during the rehearsals of *Peter Pan* in Los Angeles back in 1954.

Born in Fulham, England, she emigrated with her family to Australia when she was an infant. As a child, she was enrolled in a ballet school run by Mrs. Minnie Hooper, who recalled Madge as dainty, pretty and energetic. Her dancing career began by age thirteen with a children's ballet company in Melba, Australia.

Looking for a dance partner for Madge, Mrs. Hooper found Cyril Ritchard, a tall handsome actor who, alas, had not yet learned to dance at that stage of his life. The notion of a partnership was rekindled in 1918, and "Madge and Cyril" made a big hit in two musicals, *Yes, Uncle* and *Going Up.*

Remarkably, they soon split and didn't work together again until 1927, when they starred as dance partners in *Lady Luck,* produced in London. 1932 brought them back to Australia—becoming famous and very popular—appearing in a number of musicals.

Cyril and Madge married on September 16, 1935 at St. Mary's Cathedral in Sydney. Her wedding dress was a creation of Peter Russell, boasting a spectacular veil and train never before seen. Thousands lined the street outside the Cathedral to witness the event.

When interviewed weeks later about their wedding, Cyril proclaimed in his inimitable style, "We had a ten-year whirlwind courtship."

Madge and Cyril

Cyril & Madge's Wedding at St. Mary's Cathedral,
Sydney, Australia, September 16, 1935

Their fame in Australia became legendary, but London was calling. The couple spent the latter part of their career performing in Great Britain. In addition to an apartment in London, they purchased a cottage in the country, "Appletrees," near Kent, England.

Madge gave birth to a son in 1939 who did not survive. In the short period I knew her, and in all the years I spent with Cyril until his death in 1977, their child was never mentioned.

But why should the subject come up? Oblivious to their loss, I simply became part of their life along the way; and, perhaps significantly for them (consciously or unconsciously), I was born the same year as their son, 1939. When I came into Cyril and Maddie's life I was fourteen; and in retrospect, I can say without question that I became the son they had lost.

By chance, Cyril and Madge had been asked in 1949 to travel to New York to perform in a three-act comedy, *The Relapse.* This event launched another career in New York for Cyril.

As it turned out, Madge was facing a serious health challenge. On August 8, 1955, she died of myeloma at the age of 58. Sadly, it was one month shy of their twentieth wedding anniversary. By then, *Peter Pan* had closed on Broadway, and I was back in California attending school.

BACKSTAGE VISITORS

VICE PRESIDENT RICHARD NIXON came to see *Peter Pan* with a group of his colleagues. After the performance, the Vice President was ushered through the theatre dressing rooms, meeting everyone and shaking hands along the way. Each one of the Lost Boys was introduced to Nixon by name and we were duly impressed. "Hey, the Vice President!"

The following evening, Nixon returned with his wife Pat and their daughter Trish. Again, they were ushered into our dressing rooms after the show, and an extraordinary thing happened. Nixon introduced each of the Lost Boys to his family by name. *Wow, that was impressive.*

The Winter Garden Theatre has a long staircase from the stage door to the first floor dressing rooms and every night my mother stood at the bottom of those stairs waiting for me. As the Nixon family descended the staircase, Nixon walked straight up to my mother, took her hand and said, "You were wonderful, thank you so much!" How to spoil an illusion: my mother had nothing to do with the show. But, when all is said and done, the Vice President did remember the names of all the Lost Boys!

***

On another evening, the Lost Boys were summoned to Mary Martin's dressing room to meet Helen Keller, who had lost her sight and hearing from an illness at nineteen months old. Now at 74, she was a petite woman with a great smile. We were told to ask her any question we liked whereupon she would place her fingers gently over our mouths as we spoke.

"If you can't see and you can't hear," I asked, "how did you know what was happening on stage?" She took her hand from my lips and smiled again, "Vibrations, I feel the vibrations!" I remember her as if it were yesterday. She was glowing.

MARY MARTIN AND THE LOST BOYS: *(clockwise from front)*
Alan Sutherland (Twin); Darryl Duran (Twin); Joseph Stafford
(Michael); Stan Stenner (Curly); Mary; David Bean
(Slightly Soiled); Paris Theodore (Nibs); Inty Tucker (Tootles).

PETER PAN
NBC Live Telecast, 1955

A T THE END OF THE BROADWAY RUN, we did the first live telecast of *Peter Pan* at NBC Studio in Brooklyn. At the time, Disney Studios owned the film rights to *Peter Pan* and NBC's only option was to broadcast live and in living color. The excitement was non-stop.

Watching Mary Martin "fly" the length of this enormous studio in Brooklyn was special. Peter Foy, an Englishman, who "flew" everyone who was anyone, owned the company and on occasion would strap us into a harness and fly us around. Only the Darling family—Michael, John and Wendy—along with Peter Pan, flew in the Broadway production.

Peter Foy and his wife Babs kept in touch with me for years after the show closed. They settled in Las Vegas where "flying" was in huge demand in many of the Vegas extravaganzas. Their children continued the family's highly successful business, "Flying by Foy."

Shortly after the telecast, we boarded another Santa Fe Railroad train and returned home to Los Angeles.

~ 3 ~

Interlude

THE PLAYER'S RING THEATRE

"Heidi"

IT WASN'T LONG after *Peter Pan* closed that I auditioned for a children's musical of *Heidi,* written and directed by Kathleen Freeman. We played in the tiny Player's Ring Theatre in Hollywood. A beautiful small theatre-in-the-round, it allowed actors to literally be with the audience. It was very intimate, and we made our entrances through the audience.

I played *Peter* the goatherd to Marlyn Mason's *Heidi.* The cast was comprised of bit-part movie actors you may have seen in countless movies; but you'd never know their names. Kathleen Freeman didn't become well known until a year or two before her death in 2001. She was in over 150 movies portraying maids, nurses, teachers, secretaries and busy-bodies.

"Peter" the goatherd
in Heidi

Among the movies in which she appeared over the years were: *The Seven Year Itch; The Nutty Professor; The Sting;* and *Hocus Pocus.* She was the phonetics teacher in the 1952 film *Singin' in the Rain.* Ultimately, she made a name for herself doing the Broadway musical *The Full Monty,* for which she was nominated for a Tony Award; she also won a Theatre World Award for her role in that show.

"Johnny Appleseed"

JOHNNY APPLESEED was the second musical I did, playing the lead, also at the Player's Ring Theatre. Both *Johnny Appleseed* and *Heidi* played only on the weekends as children's shows and were so much fun.

At times, the lights would come up on a scene and there sitting beside you on a bench was a small child from the audience. *How do you handle that?* Well, I would give him an appleseed and have him go back to his seat, seed in hand, thus making him a part of the play.

TAKE TWO!

Cyril: "Encore!"

Live Telecast of Peter Pan, 1956

CYRIL RITCHARD made a surprise visit to see *Johnny Appleseed*. After the performance, he asked if I would like to fly back to New York City with him to do the second live telecast of *Peter Pan* at the NBC Studio in Brooklyn. So, with my parents' enthusiastic consent, my very first airplane ride was with "Captain Hook" on a Lockheed Constellation four-engine propeller airplane. Today, this beautiful relic is affectionately called "Connie." It could fly from LA to New York in seven hours. *Wow, the next thing you know, they'll be flying to the moon.*

BON VOYAGE: *Dad and Mom watch from the Los Angeles Airport tarmac as I take off for NYC on my first flight.*

Cyril's apartment in Manhattan was just yards away from Bonwit Teller, the luxury department store at Fifth Avenue and 56th Street. How super convenient not to have to worry about getting to the NBC Studio in Brooklyn. I simply went to work with "Captain Hook"!

Every morning after breakfast, one of us had to wash the dishes. "Your turn, dear boy," Cyril informed me on one particular day, with his clear Aussie accent.

"No, no, I washed up yesterday."

"Nonsense," he said, and playfully grabbed me around the neck to push me into the kitchen. I resisted and managed to pick him up off the floor. *(Whoa, he's six-foot four, and 260 pounds!)* We both fell over.

Cyril, trying to catch himself, fell backward breaking his big toe. *My God, his toe is turning vivid colors and swelling. I can't believe I just broke "Captain Hook's" big toe!*

There wasn't anything we could do, so we simply drove out to NBC Studio in Brooklyn — to prepare for the final dress rehearsal scheduled before the live telecast that evening. Everyone made such a fuss when we arrived; a numbing spray was ordered and the run-through started.

Cyril must have been in great pain. Just to get his Pirate boots on had to be excruciating. *But the show must go on.*

In the second act, the Pirates and *Captain Hook* were on the ship and *Peter Pan,* dressed up like a Pirate, infiltrates his scurvy crew. At one point, *Peter* is on a Pirate's back. During the *Pirate Song,* she jumps from the Pirate's back, landing on Cyril's (broken) toe.

It was very fortunate that this was the dress rehearsal, as the show came to an abrupt halt. Cyril was quickly ushered to a chair and his boot was removed.

It seemed to be a miracle! Landing full force on his big toe had disbursed all the blood-clotted portions of his swollen toe, thus relieving the pain. Good thing! *I'm now off the hook and the real "Hook" can do the live telecast free of any pain.* (Well, mostly pain-free.)

The live telecast was a great success. As it happened, the 1956 performance (as was true with the 1955 live telecast), was not put on film. Disney still owned the film rights. But a kinescope of each performance did survive — a kinescope which you can purchase on disc today. Most of the color is gone, but it's still fun to see. Those original live telecasts in 1955 and 1956 were both directed by Jerome Robbins.

A Week

in the Hamptons

SHORTLY AFTER the second live NBC telecast of *Peter Pan,* Cyril and I were invited to the luxury estate of Elaine Carrington in Bridgehampton, Long Island. In the City, Cyril and I were frequent dinner guests at Elaine's apartment in Manhattan. And I well remember escorting her to the opening night of *No Time for Sergeants,* starring Andy Griffith.

Mrs. Carrington's invitation to her country estate was for the entire week, which would allow The Boss (a.k.a. Cyril) to enjoy some well-deserved R & R. Elaine was a very successful writer of radio soaps (including *Pepper Young's Family*), TV dramas, and a Broadway play. Her home was palatial and right on Long Island Sound.

This was going to be a stupendous week, as she had plans for us that would keep us from getting bored. Hearing this, The Boss put on a Cheshire cat smile all through Elaine's dissertation of what she thought might entertain us.

But first we had to meet Eliza, as well as Seekie and Ram. Eliza was Elaine's full-time cook; Seekie and Ram were her canine companions. Little did we know how very well-acquainted we would become with Eliza, as she eventually came to work and live at Cyril's new apartment on Central Park West, where she took care of both of us after Madge's death.

Seekie and Ram were beautiful, young, well-trained black standard poodles, who loved sharing the enormous plush sofa with everyone. It didn't take long for Cyril to relax, sharing the sofa with Elaine, me, and the dogs.

One morning, our hostess waltzed into the living room, plopping herself between her dogs and us, and announced, "I have a delightful surprise for this evening." I'm sure Cyril was looking forward to a quiet dinner on the terrace, cooked by Eliza, then a restful evening and an early night. "We have guests coming this evening to celebrate your brilliant successful telecast of *Peter Pan*. Won't that be fun?"

Cyril, putting his finger to his chin, gave me a puzzled look of dismay, and the only sound I heard was, "Oh, dear!" I could read his mind. This was meant to be a week in the country, quiet and restful.

The Cheshire cat smile returned as he responded to Elaine, "Lovely, dear. Do I know them?"

"I think you do, dear," was her reply.

"Let's see," she continued, "there is Eli Wallach and the Mrs. [actress Anne Jackson]. And you surely know Kermit Bloomgarden don't you, darling? He's the wonderful producer, you know, *Death of a Salesman* and *The Diary of Anne Frank,* and some other very important shows."

She was on a roll and couldn't be stopped.

"Arthur Miller and his new bride, you know, Marilyn? And, lest we forget our young Master David here, I've invited a very nice young girl his age, named Mimsey. I think you two will get along fabulously."

My eyes met Cyril's as he said, "Marilyn?" And I added, "Monroe?" Cyril's eyebrows went up and his Cheshire cat smile turned immediately to a grin. This was the promise of an electric evening. We were not let down.

Eli Wallach and Anne Jackson were charming and talked theatre with Cyril. And my new cohort Mimsey and I plied Dom Perignon to each of the arriving guests.

When Arthur Miller and Marilyn Monroe arrived, the party clearly stepped up a notch. You could not help but notice the energy of Marilyn the moment she stepped through the front door. She was drop-dead gorgeous. Clinging to her newlywed husband, they toured the room greeting everyone, as Mimsey and I continued with the champagne deliveries.

Elaine put on some dance music and it was no surprise that our hostess invited me on to the floor and we began to dance. Marilyn made her way over to us, cutting in on Elaine, and we started to jitterbug. Her movements were sensuous and exciting. Cyril commented later on how professional we looked. My comment to him was, "Duh, that's the profession we're in, ain't it?" Secretly, I thought to myself, what fun it was dancing with the world-famous Marilyn Monroe. Both of us showing off — to a small but appreciative audience.

CROSS COUNTRY
1956

WHEN I TURNED SIXTEEN on December 4, 1955, I was back home in California. And I beat a path to the Motor Vehicle Department, anxious to pass my driver's test. First time out, I flunked. Thirty in a 25 mph zone was an automatic failure. Three weeks later, I kept the car under the speed limit, and my license was in the bag.

I received a call from Cyril with a request to fly back to New York City and help him drive to California in his 1941 Chrysler. We set out from New York with a few rules. A half hour of rock-and-roll (my choice), and a half hour of news or classical music (The Boss's choice). Each of us would drive 100 miles and then switch places.

Six hundred miles per day would allow time to rest, eat well, and find a church for Cyril to attend Mass every morning before plodding on. We didn't speed and the Chrysler performed very nicely all the way to Arizona.

In Phoenix, we got an early morning start and were about one hundred miles west into the Mojave Desert when, *Pow*, we had a blowout. In minutes, I had the car jacked up and the blown out tire off. But when I tried to unbolt the spare in the trunk, I had trouble getting the lug nut loose.

Before we left, Cyril had had the spare tire checked. The mechanic had apparently used a pneumatic wrench when replacing the lug nuts. The result: one of the lug nuts was on too tight and that sucker was on to stay.

The morning was beautiful and, as one might expect, getting hotter by the minute. I couldn't budge the lug nut. What to do?

We put our heads together and realized that it would be impossible to backtrack one hundred miles to Phoenix with a blown tire. Hitchhiking ahead would be our best bet to find help. Cyril would stay with the car and I would thumb a ride to the next station. I was right. It was only fifty miles ahead. I thanked the kind driver who dropped me at a lone station in the middle of the Mojave Desert.

With only one gas attendant at this station, he couldn't really help me. But he recommended that I call ahead to the next town and get help from a gas station. And he kindly gave me their phone number.

I found the pay phone and, believe it or not, the phone company was on strike. It took twenty minutes to get a phone executive to connect me with the station. *Eureka, at last!*

It was agreed…a mechanic would drive out, pick me up and take me back to what might possibly be a fresh-roasted Cyril in the front seat of a pale blue '41 Chrysler. It was 2 p.m. when we found Cyril sitting in the Chrysler with his cravat still in place. He was soaking wet, but very proper. I would have been stripped to my skivvies in this heat!

Our rescuer, driving a souped-up pickup, jumped out and quickly surveyed the scene. "OK, I got this," he said, as he disappeared to the rear of his pickup. He reappeared empty-handed but, more noticeably, bearing a vacant look on his face.

"What?" I asked.

"I didn't bring my tool box!" said the mechanic sheepishly. "I have no tools. You got a lug nut wrench?"

So I gave him the wrench that came with the car. Jumping into the trunk, he began grunting like crazy trying to loosen the nuts that were holding fast to the spare wheel.

"Can't get it," he moaned.

In the front seat of his truck, he found a hammer and chisel.

"I can knock those nuts off with the chisel and you'll be off and running." He climbed back into the trunk with his hammer and chisel. Placing the chisel behind the base of the lug nut he swung his hammer as hard as he could. The hammer hit the tire and bounced back like a shot hitting our rescuer in the forehead, knocking him out cold! There we were, in the middle of the desert with a disabled vehicle on the side of the road and a disabled mechanic out cold in our trunk.

Within minutes, he came around and Cyril was gallantly giving up his cravat to stop the bleeding on the chap's forehead. It was nearly 4 pm, time to come up with an alternate solution.

Revised plan: we would pile into his pickup truck with the souped-up Olds engine; take the blown tire with us to his station 75 miles ahead. We would stay the night and return in the morning with a new tire on the rim. It was pushing 105 degrees and the alternative of dying in the desert was not appealing. Luggage was piled into the pickup and we squeezed into the truck — three across.

The key turned in the ignition. Rumble, rumble! Again, rumble, rumble. Oh crap, the truck with its hot Olds engine would not start!

All this time, I'm astounded that Cyril, with all his Australian majesty, had barely said a word. "Captain Hook" should surely be at a point of outrage. *"Rip up his gusset and down his sash, and slash his aft and fore. Then pass the finger bowl, Charlie, we'll all dip our hands in the gore"* — or our auto mechanic, whichever comes first! It did take another half hour and three pints of sweat before we were off to the next town, 75 miles ahead.

Much to our relief, we were successfully reunited the following morning with our blue Chrysler and managed to carry on to California without further mishaps. A sunny day by the pool in Palm Springs was out. *Pity!*

HAWAII

Summer 1956

"HOW WOULD YOU LIKE to go on a trip to Hawaii?" Cyril asked with a gleam in his eyes and his predictable Cheshire cat smile. "I've got time off and a vacation is in order," he continued.

"Are you kidding?" was my enthusiastic reply.

"Meet me at Saks Fifth Avenue in Hollywood. We have to get you some proper clothes. We've been invited to a dinner dance. So it would be appropriate to be properly dressed," he suggested.

That's how a trip of a lifetime was born. I had no idea what to expect. We met at Saks and I was fitted with a white dinner jacket, black trousers with a stripe up both sides of my legs, a very nice frilly dress shirt, and patent leather shoes. . . . I was ready to meet the Queen.

Our flight left Los Angeles early morning in a very large Strata Clipper. The belly of the plane was a bar. For the 1950s, this plane was enormous. Four prop engines were loud on takeoff but settled down as we established our heading to the islands. Cyril fell asleep within a short period of time and I wandered down to the bar. I was told another flight to Hawaii preceded ours, explaining the empty seats on our flight.

"Do you have any hot chocolate?" I asked the steward. I was the only passenger in the bar and the steward and I spent a couple of hours depleting the hot chocolate supply. I wandered back to my seat to find Cyril in a rather snippy mood. I inquired about his nap, and he gave me a tongue-lashing for leaving him. I didn't pay much attention as the poor man must have really needed a few days off. We had lunch and he fell back asleep. As we were near the islands, I was invited up to the cockpit with the pilots. I sat on an apple box between the captain and his co-pilot. Imagine having an apple box in the cockpit of a super modern airplane. I sat there for the entire approach to Honolulu and landing. It was spectacular describing this to Cyril who was still a little peeved with me for leaving him alone the first time. I noticed his Cheshire cat smile had been missing for some time. He must be really tired.

Royal Hawaiian Hotel, 1956

Our digs were the very pink Royal Hawaiian Hotel on Waikiki Beach. Our suite had a "Lanai" (screened porch) overlooking the beach. Flowers and a spectacular tray of fresh pineapple greeted our arrival. It was magic. To get our bearings, we took a walk on the beach along the shore. Passing a small cottage very near the water, Cyril stopped and pointed to the cottage.

"Maddie and I spent our honeymoon in that cottage," he said, then continued to describe the memory of waking up in the middle of the night and watching his wife sleep with the moonlight streaming in across her beautiful face. He was transported to Never-Never Land. It was a rare moment to see him so nostalgic and emotional.

We spent the following day on the beach. He left me to surf and hang out while he had a lunch date with whom, I can't remember. I struck up a conversation with a kid on the beach who turned out to be the son of General MacArthur. We had great fun as we ogled the women on the beach and lamented we were here with very adult supervision which totally cramped our style.

Returning to the room, it was time to prepare for the formal evening of dining and dancing. Both of us arrived at the party looking very dapper, Cyril in black tie and me in my white dinner jacket. Our table included our hosts and, to my surprise, a cute sixteen-year-old . . . my date. She was a sweet girl who loved to dance. And dance we did. There was a very big band and we nearly wore out the floor.

The evening was a big success. Cyril and I arrived back at the hotel exhausted. Just as I was about to remove my beautiful white dinner jacket

I happened to see myself in a full-length mirror. I could not believe what I saw. How could I have missed it? All the way down the front of my very handsome white dinner jacket was chocolate ice cream. I asked The Boss, "Did you see this?"

"Of course, dear boy," he replied, "but people were watching you two dance. I dare say you had a marvelous time."

The following day, we were driven back to the airport and were seated in a McDonald Douglas DC3 airplane, an old tail-dragger used to move tourists from one island to the other. Our destination was the tiny island of Lanai. The Dole Pineapple Corporation owned the entire island, I was told. A small village, set 800 feet above the valley of the island, experienced a twenty percent temperature change. *Refreshing!* There was a small nine-hole golf course and a tiny theatre with very uncomfortable wooden chairs should you want to see a movie.

The population was ninety percent plantation workers, nine percent Mormon missionaries, and the two of us. We were given a '40s army Jeep to use for getting from the village to the beach. Under the seats was a large machete needed when passing through the pineapple fields — just in case you wanted a fresh piece of fruit.

Early the first morning, I dressed and went to the golf course, rented a bag of clubs, and played nine holes. Upon my return, I thought The Boss would surely be up and about and we could go for breakfast.

But Cyril wasn't there when I arrived back at the room. *The Boss had gone.* He had simply packed his suitcase and left me on the island.

Oh brother, what did I do now? Of course, I didn't think he would want to play golf. I left him to rest, which was the sole purpose of this whole trip. But the fact was that I left him alone!

I had no idea the stress he was under. Maddie had just passed and he was out there in limbo, terrified of being alone. I understand that now, but only years later. At sixteen, I certainly was no seasoned psychoanalyst. This was a very emotional journey for Cyril and unfortunately, I didn't have a clue.

Cyril

British journalist chronicles amazing young career of American teenager

"**D**AVID BEAN has achieved the rare feat of playing in top productions in both New York and London before the age of 20. .... He first reached Broadway in the outstanding production of *Peter Pan* with Mary Martin. At the age of fourteen, he was a juvenile star in a show on Broadway. ... In the first London production of *West Side Story*, David had to act, sing and dance — a test for any talent — as "Big Deal," one of the leading members of the Jets. He met some of the most famous names in London, including Princess Margaret, an enthusiastic admirer of *West Side Story*, and Noel Coward, whom David first met on Broadway. ... He had also been in an outstanding production of Offenbach's opera *La Périchole* in Central City, Colorado and Hollywood. ... By 19, he was what London theatre men call 'an old trouper' or a real 'pro.' "

— *February 5, 1959*

WILLIAM WEATHERBY
journalist and author

Bill Weatherby is the author of biographies of James Baldwin, Marilyn Monroe, and Jackie Gleason. He also penned the book *Chariots of Fire,* based on the original screenplay. Born in England, he wrote on both sides of the pond for the *Manchester Guardian, New York Times, Washington Post* and *Newsweek.*

~ 4 ~

West Side Story

(London Production)

Prologue to our British Adventure

Was it meant to be?

FATE had a lot to do with my being in any production of *West Side Story*. I was in New York City just after the original Broadway opening in 1957, as was my sister Janet. She had just returned from a trip to Europe and I was there to start rehearsals for the Summer Tour with the Metropolitan Opera Ballet in *La Périchole,* a French comic opera. We decided to take in a Broadway show and we got tickets to *West Side Story.*

I will never forget the impact that show had on me. The opening scene with the Jets sitting on the steps at the beginning of the *Prologue* will be forever etched in my memory. I left the theatre enthralled, and remember saying to my sister, "Wow, wouldn't it be great to be in that show?"

By January of '58, producers Robert Griffith and Harold Prince wanted to take *West Side Story* across the pond to London. Their idea was to replace Chita Rivera in the Broadway production sending her to London. By chance, a romance between Chita and Tony Mordente was in full bloom, and they married December 1, 1957. Tony was a member of the cast, playing the part of *A-Rab,* a member of the Jets. To start rehearsals in March of '58, the new production could open in the West End of London by May. Chita agreed to leave the show until she announced she was with child, her due date near August. Because Griffith and Prince wanted Chita in their production, they made plans to start rehearsals in September, postponing the entire production until Chita had her baby (Little Lisa) and was able to resume dancing.

Was this fate? I was dancing in San Bernardino in a musical *Plain and Fancy* and would not have been available to travel to London had Jerry called me in the Spring of '58. By June, I was in rehearsals with the Metropolitan Opera production of *La Périchole* which didn't end until late August. Jerry Robbins called me in September and the rest is history. However, the mystery remains. *Had Chita not been pregnant, would Jerry have called 10 months earlier than he did? And if he had, would I have been able to leave the show I was under contract with?* Happily, we will never know.

New York, 1958

Returning home from *Peter Pan* in 1956, I had another year of high school. As it turned out, my agent, Milton Goldman, was contacted by Jerry Robbins for a new musical he was putting together, *West Side Story.* Jerry asked, "Is David available?"

"David is in Los Angeles," Milton told him, "getting his high school diploma and isn't doing any shows till he graduates." So I missed the auditions for the opportunity to be in the original Broadway production of *West Side Story;* in fact, I never knew until 1958 when Jerry called me personally and asked if I had graduated.

In the fall of 1958, auditions for the London production of *West Side Story* were being held in New York City at the Winter Garden Theatre, on 50th and Broadway. Jerry was wondering if I could fly out to be there.

I was quite familiar with the Winter Garden Theatre; we had played there in *Peter Pan.* The audition went smoothly. Surprisingly, I wasn't nervous and I had fun. It really felt like old home week.

Choreographers Howard Jeffrey and Tommy Abbott assisted Jerry Robbins with the auditions, and after each dance sequence the dancers were separated. Jerry would send some of the dancers home and those of us left would start all over with new dance combinations.

I spent four days auditioning and didn't hear a word. No one called and I thought, *Well, that's that.* I packed my bag and flew home, more than a little disappointed.

The following day, Jerry called me directly — and he couldn't believe I went home. When he told me to fly back to New York the very next day, I could hear that signature giggle-laugh in his voice. Rehearsals would be starting on the following Monday for the London production of *West Side Story.*

When we arrived to start rehearsals at the Alvin Theatre, it was dark and empty. Jerry decided to rehearse the entire show at the Alvin. And by the time we flew to England, the show was pretty much put together.

Rehearsals in New York were beastly. When I started, I weighed in at 170 pounds; after the first week, I was down to 150. I needed some good home-cooked meals.

ENTER ELIZA

DURING THESE *West Side Story* rehearsal days in the City, I had the good fortune of living at Cyril's apartment on Central Park West. One special treat in this arrangement was that my meals were prepared by Cyril's cook, Eliza. At the time, Cyril himself was in Australia.

Every night, Eliza would cook my dinner and place it on the hunting table that looked into the living room. We watched TV while we ate.

As it turned out, I was blessed to have Eliza as my "mother" away from home. Born in the West Indies, she never grew much taller than 4'10". Appropriately enough, her name was Eliza Small.

We had many deals in our living arrangements. I could have rock-and-roll on the radio, but on the hour she could listen to the news. If a peppy Elvis song was on the radio, we would jitterbug in the living room. I had to get my own breakfast because *she wasn't going to wake up for me!* I agreed to that of course, but I never did end up doing any of my own cooking for breakfast, lunch or dinner. She had command of the kitchen. "You get your own cooking, David." But contrary to her stern words, I never did.

She was fond of bossing me around, and was responsible for my table etiquette—how to set a table, which pieces of silverware to use and when to use them. And if I messed up, I heard more stern words. She would assign me various household chores. One day, she pulled me by my ear, dragging me into my bedroom.

"What?" I'd ask.

"Turn the mattress for me," she said. Yes, she acted as if she were my mom — and enjoyed every minute of it. At dinner, she walked behind my chair from the kitchen to serve. As she passed behind me going back into the kitchen, she would affectionately smack the back of my head with the back of her hand.

When Cyril was at home, breakfast was at 9 a.m. sharp. Eliza rang a bell if I was late. Cyril would sit at the table with a straight back with both hands on the table waiting to be served. His demeanor was always the same, formal. One morning I had the brilliant idea of changing postures with The Boss. He would slump in his chair while I would sit erect with both hands on the table. Eliza entered the room with a pause in her step—just enough to take in what we were up to. As usual, she walked to Cyril first and waited while he slopped the eggs onto his plate making a deliberate mess. Eliza said nothing, even pretended not to notice. She walked to my end of the table and set the hot platter on my hand. "Get your hands off the table," she said, smacking me playfully on the back of the head as she returned to the kitchen.

Keeping me healthy was her main goal. If not for Eliza, the rigors of dancing and working under Jerome Robbins would have been overwhelming. As a pair, we were much more than a cook and a casual houseguest. I adored that woman, and she adored me. *My "mom" away from home.*

JEROME (JERRY) ROBBINS

KNOWN AS A TASKMASTER, Jerome Robbins was living up to his reputation. But with the exception of Jerry's outburst during a run-through of *Peter Pan* at age fourteen, I personally was never at the short end of his temper—mainly because I never did anything to tick him off. Jerry still maintained his infectious giggle-laugh, especially in class.

Work on the ballet barre was part of our routine everyday before rehearsals and that's when you could make Jerry laugh. He was the inventor of half-hour class before half-hour. It counted as rehearsal time so you had to be there. The show was physical to say the least and it was smart to warm up before each show. He made it mandatory. Robbins was a method actor in dance and required an equal emotional dimension that ultimately changed the technical appearance of each step. He was adamant when he came out with, "I want you to dance like you're inside a paper bag and you're desperate to get out. Show me the emotion. I don't want a TV dancer."

We were rehearsing the dance number *Cool,* and at one point the music went *da*... two three four, *da*... two three four, *da*... two three four — *da*!!! Full stop and we all would freeze. On the last *"da"* I froze and pulled every muscle in my back. I lost my breath; the lightning bolt pain put me on the floor with a horrific gasp. I was sent to the hospital and they sent me back to rehearsal all taped up like a mummy.

Jerry asked how I felt; I said I was stiff from all the tape! "Tape?" he exclaimed, "They taped you up"? I took off my shirt and sure enough I looked like a mummy. "They can't tape up a pulled muscle," he said — and proceeded to rip off all the tape. Actually, it felt a little better, but it was painful to dance. "Use it," Jerry exhorted. "If you think you have a knife in your back, use it. You're a Jet and it's painful. Use it!"

Afterward, I was sent to a chiropractor named Dr. Bachrach. A chiropractor named "Bachrach"? You just can't make up this stuff. At the time, Dr. Bachrach was the chiropractor to most dancers in New York City. This was in the '50s when chiropractors were not considered doctors. We didn't care about their title. All we knew was that chiropractors kept most dancers on their feet, as they do to this day!

WEST SIDE STORY "COOL" REHEARSALS AT THE ALVIN THEATER, NYC
(l. to r.) Tony Mordente, George Chakiris, Jerome Robbins,
Eddie Verso, Gary Cockrell, Sylvia Tysick and me. September 1958

FLIGHT
TO
ENGLAND

The cast had to pack up and fly to England. We were flying a Pan Am special charter. "WEST SIDE STORY" was painted above the door, and we felt very special as we boarded. Each of us was given a travel bag with a Pan Am logo on one side, and West Side Story on the other. It was a perfect rehearsal bag for later use.

Everyone connected with the show was on board. Producers Griffith and Prince, the entire cast, of course, and all of Jerry's assistants, Tommy Abbott, Howard Jeffrey and Dee Dee Wood, Betty Walberg (our pianist), and Ruth Mitchell (general manager), who later became co-producer for future Broadway shows. Champagne was flowing; it was indeed a party. Our dinner menu was catered by Maxim's of Paris. Very posh.

On November 8, 1958, we landed in foggy Manchester. England was burning coal at the time and Manchester was covered in smog—coal smog. We were there less than a day when everyone was forced to wear masks to breathe. The cold was another thing. It was damp and chilly all the time. Ten blankets on your bed couldn't keep the damp cold out! The hotel was without heat and, yes, damp! The Opera House in Manchester was also without heat. They would open the outer door for the public to enter and all the smog would fill the theatre. From the stage, you could barely see the audience.

On December 6, we were put on one of those lovely English trains and transported to London. As the train pulled out of the station, we were all excited to have a day off, and to have it on this British treasure in comfort, spending our first night at a hotel in London . . . with heat.

WELCOME ABOARD

Gloria, Eddie, Maureen, Mark, Lina, me

ACT II

WESTSIDE STORY MENU

Canapes
Cheese Wafers
Salted Nuts — Olives

Shrimp Cocktail

Choice of:
Grilled Filet Mignon Maitre d'Hotel
or
Rock Cornish Game Hen a la President
or
Lobster Americaine — Pilaff Rice
Asparagus Tips   Baked Potatoes

PAN AMERICAN
WORLD'S MOST EXPERIENCED AIRLINE

Portions of the 8-page program given to all of the West Side Story passengers on our memorable (and fun!) Nov. 7, 1958 flight.

Passenger List

THE JETS

Riff, the Leader....GEORGE CHAKIRIS
Tony, his friend..............DON McKAY
Action ....EDDIE ROLL
A-Rab ....TONY MORDENTE
Baby John ....ED VERSO
Snowboy ....RIGGS O'HARA
Big Deal ....DAVID BEAN
Diesel ....GARY COCKERELL
Gee-Tar ....MICHEL KLEINMAN
Mouthpiece ....JOE DONOVAN
Tiger ....GLEN GIBSON

THE SHARKS

Bernardo, Leader..............KEN Le ROY
Maria, his sister ....MARLYS WATTERS
Anita, his girl ....CHITA RIVERA
Chino ....BEN GERARD
Pepe ....KEITH STEWART
Indio ....MARC SCOTT
Luis ....DON PERCASSI
Anxious ....LEO KHARIBIAN
Nibbles ....BUD FLEMING
Juano ....BILLY WILSON

THEIR GIRLS

Graziella ....LESLIE FRANZOS
Velma ....SUSAN WATSON
Minnie ....INGE ROLL
Clarice ....MAUREEN GILLICK
Anybodys ....SYLVIA TYSICK

THEIR GIRLS

Rosalia ....FRANCESCA BELL
Teresita ....YVONNE OTHON
Francisca ....GLORIA HIGDON
Estella ....ROBERTA KEITH
Marguerita ....LINA SORIANO

THE ADULTS

Doc ....DAVID BAUER
Schrank ....TED GUNTHER
Krupke ....HAL GALILI
Gladhand ....DAVID HOLLIDAY

Cuisine By	*Aircraft By*
MAXIM'S OF PARIS	**DOUGLAS AIRCRAFT CO.**

HER MAJESTY REGRETS

CENSORSHIP IN THE ENGLISH THEATRE

D URING THE HUSTLE of endless preparations for the opening night in London, the cast and orchestra, along with the crew, were not the only ones subject to last minute details. In the United Kingdom, you were subject to the Lord Chamberlain, the most senior officer of the Royal Household, giving his approval of the script.

Abolition of censorship in the English theatre, a law established in 1843, took place in 1969. That was eleven years after *West Side Story* opened at Her Majesty's Theatre in the West End of London. It was the Royal prerogative to apply censorship in theatre productions on behalf of Her Majesty the Queen by the Lord Chamberlain. Hence, we were subject to the Lord Chamberlain's approval before we opened. Gathered at a prearranged meeting were the American producers, Robert Griffith and Harold Prince, along with Hugh "Binkie" Beaumont, head of H.M. Tennent Ltd., the English producer. Jerome Robbins also attended this meeting and told us this story.

The Lord Chamberlain was seated at the head of the table. An open copy of the *West Side Story* script sat before him from which he was reading aloud to the rest of the dignitaries seated at this enormously long conference table. The first act went smoothly as was expected, as would the second act — until he arrived at the song *Gee, Officer Krupke*. The Lord Chamberlain began very slowly, pronouncing each word of the song with a labored, but exquisite, English accent.

My father is a bosstard.

His bushy eyebrows went straight up to his hairline, but he slowly continued:

My ma's an S. O. B.
My grandpa's always plosstered.
My grandma pushes tea.
(Then a long pause.)

My sister wears a mustache.
My brother wears a dress.
Goodness gracious, that's why I'm a mess. . . .

He stopped, puckered his lips, stroked his ear lobe, and quite seriously asked, "What does pushing tea mean?"

In the end, everything received the Lord Chamberlain's approval — with one exception. The tomboy *Anybodys'* line, "You bet your fat A" was changed to "You bet your fat butt."

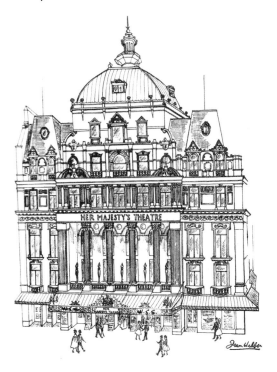

HER MAJESTY'S THEATRE

OPENING NIGHT came on December 12th at Her Majesty's Theatre at the bottom of the Haymarket, in the West End. In the wings, all of the Jets were on set, ready for the opening scene as we listened to the overture. Our hearts were pounding and the air was filled with anticipation. There was loud applause as the curtain rose and the *Prologue* began.

West Side Story turned out to be an instant smash hit. There were endless curtain calls as the night seemed to go on forever. The excitement was truly unforgettable. Jerry was a very happy man. A reception was held in the foyer of the theatre after the show.

David and Jerry Robbins at the opening night reception in London, December 12, 1958

"David Bean! David Bean!" A chap was walking through the crowd calling my name. It was Binkie Beaumont, the British theatre manager and producer.

"My name is Mr. Beaumont, David. Noel Coward would like to talk with you."

"Really?" I said, "And what do you do, Mr. Beaumont?" I asked. At that moment I had no idea who he was.

"I'm your boss, follow me!"

Binkie Beaumont is to London what David Merrick is to Broadway. In fact, Binkie was *the* most famous and controversial figure in the history of British theatre. Although David Merrick could not make that claim on this side of the pond, he was, after all, a prolific Tony Award-winning American theatrical producer.

As best as I could figure it all out, Noel Coward must have seen Cyril in New York City and mentioned he was going to see *West Side*

Story in London. Cyril must have suggested that he look me up. It didn't seem likely that Mr. Coward would have remembered meeting me onstage at the Winter Garden Theater in New York City three years earlier when I was performing in *Peter Pan.*

In any event, we had a nice chat. I asked why he was in London, and he replied, "Nothing at all, dear boy. I have nothing to do for one whole glorious week."

"Well, I make a great leg of lamb. If you're free Sunday, please join George Chakiris and me for dinner."

"How gracious, dear boy, I accept!"

So there I was, eighteen years old, in a hit West End show in London, with a super flat just behind Buckingham Palace, and now booked to cook a leg of lamb for Noel Coward.

The evening got even better when a few of us decided to search out where we might buy a late-evening edition of the London papers for the opening night reviews. We walked up to Piccadilly Circus and accosted a young couple just getting out of a taxi.

"Where would we find the newspapers?" we asked. They patiently explained we would have to go to the Strand and wait for the early edition.

"Where is the Strand?" we asked. We explained who we were and that we had just opened in *West Side Story* and were looking for the reviews. We couldn't wait for their answer so we simply "kidnapped" the couple and we all went to the Covent Garden near the Strand to find the papers.

As it turned out, the young couple, Jeremy and Sarah Grayson, were married that afternoon and were on their honeymoon. We kept them up all night!

Jeremy was a photographer and he fit right in, taking pictures of many of the cast later in the year; and the couple photographed our wedding as well as being our invited guests, two-and-a-half years later.

The reviews that night were brilliant—exploding throughout the London newspaper headlines. The show was locked in for a lengthy run in the West End.

About a month after we opened in London, the composer Leonard Bernstein, who had composed the score for *West Side Story,* arrived in London to see our production. We were asked to stay on stage after the performance for notes from Mr. Bernstein. Within seconds of the final curtain call, he burst through the center curtain, walked straight up to me, gave me a huge hug and said, "David, you were wonderful!" and went on to other cast members. Imagine, *Wow,* we had never met and he knew my name. Years later, I did have the pleasure of meeting his adult children, but I never personally saw "Lenny, my bud" again. That night in London, the magnificent composer did stay on stage to give us notes; but in all the excitement, I don't remember a word he said.

Not so with Arthur Laurents, who wrote the book for *West Side Story.* Once again, we all had to stay on stage after the show for notes from Mr. Laurents. This had to be six months after we opened. He actually looked quite angry walking out on stage. Jean Deeks, my future wife, was standing on stage with us. (She didn't actually join the company until the summer of '59.) Mr. Laurents was not happy with the performance that evening, telling us, "No one really listens to each other. Your responses to one another are automatic. Are any of you truly aware of each other?"

"Can anyone tell me what color socks I have on?" he challenged us, seeking to bring home the point. His tirade was instantly interrupted...

"Green and yellow," came a voice from within the cast.

"What?" he jerked to a halt obviously annoyed at the interruption.

"What?" he repeated.

"Your socks. They are green and yellow." It was a loud response from the tiny Jean Deeks.

Everyone seemed happy for this bit of comic relief, and Mr. Laurents lost his serious rampage. Was he right? Probably, but no one wanted to hear it; and Jean did save the day, as Mr. Laurents gave in with an amused smile.

George Chakiris, London, 1959

Eccleston Mews

E DGAR RITCHARD, Cyril's brother, lived in London and had arranged for me to view a mews flat near Buckingham Palace. George Chakiris *(Riff)* and I agreed to share the Eccleston Mews flat. We settled in within a couple of days. It had central heating, *ta-da!* It was expensive, seven guineas a week ($28.00), which, even in London, was quite expensive at the time. Eccleston Mews was originally built to house horses belonging to the upper class. The horses lived below and the family tending to them lived upstairs. Located near Sloane Square, and behind Buckingham Palace, Eccleston Mews was considered a very posh neighborhood.

Our flat had two bedrooms upstairs with a kitchen and bath, and large living quarters downstairs where the horses used to bunk. We had a dumbwaiter from the kitchen to the lower level that was the dining area. Outside the mews, we had a cobblestone-paved path all the way out to the street. It was absolutely charming.

It wasn't long before George and I bought bicycles to pedal ourselves to work. Out the Eccleston Mews and around Buckingham Palace down the Mall to Trafalgar Square, hang a left and

Me, London, 1959

you are at the Haymarket and Her Majesty's Theatre. A twenty minute ride that proved faster than an English taxi. There were nights, however, when we had to walk the bikes as the London fog was thick as pea soup; you couldn't see three feet in front of you.

We also got friendly with the Palace guards, riding alongside them as they marched back to their barracks after they changed the Guard. They weren't supposed to talk while on duty; but they were like a gaggle of boisterous geese chatting all the way back to their barracks.

Portrait by Jeremy Grayson, London, 1959

NOEL COWARD, DINNER GUEST

IT WAS SUNDAY. George Chakiris and I spent the morning getting the mews flat tidy for our special guest. We were more than excited to be hosting Noel Coward for a fabulous leg of lamb with all the fixins. I prepared a chocolate steamed pudding from a recipe Eliza (Cyril's live-in cook and my NYC mom) had slipped into my luggage when I was packing for London.

"Be sure to buy a good cookbook when you get there," she scolded in her best West Indian accent. "You are too skinny boy, you need some fat on those bones." It was in her honor I was making the steamed pudding—looking forward to telling her that Noel Coward actually ate one of her dishes.

With our kitchen upstairs and the dining area on the first floor, one had to choreograph the evening meal using the dumbwaiter. I loaded everything from the kitchen and George would be downstairs and unload the dumbwaiter to the table. The evening was set with an open bottle of red wine on the table to breathe. I was probably more excited about preparing the roast lamb than having company. At eighteen, I hardly knew who Noel Coward was, except for the stories Cyril had told over dinner.

During World War II, Cyril and Madge lived in London's Grosvenor Square and worked with a circle of theatrical friends that included Ivor Novello, Gertrude Lawrence, Jack Buchanan, Gladys Cooper, Bea Lillie and, of course, Noel Coward. Putting on shows during The Blitz was what they did, and the stories Cyril told were horrific. Cyril and Maddie's apartment in Grosvenor Square was bombed, splitting their apartment in half. The Steinway grand piano was left hanging from the second floor. Cyril was quick to have it removed before the building was condemned.

Noel Coward

The moment had arrived. There was a knock at the door, and enter stage right, the man of the hour. George greeted our guest and we all settled in the living area with drinks in hand.

"This is absolutely charming, dear boy. How ever did you find this flat?" Noel inquired.

"Cyril's brother, Edgar," I replied.

We related the details of Edgar and his clever search for digs close to the theatre and having central heating.

"Central heating," Coward mimed. "How absolutely posh, dear boy!"

He was gracious and overwhelmed by the production of *West Side Story* and filled the room with his articulate diction and praise. I excused myself and ran upstairs to tend to the meal, loading it onto the dumbwaiter.

Everything was set on the table, from which I carved the beautiful pink leg of lamb and plated our meal. The carrots and Brussels sprouts were perfectly al dente. Crosse & Blackwell mint jelly paired perfectly with the lamb, as did the wine.

Eliza would surely have been proud of her chocolate steamed pudding, topped with brandy sauce straight out of a bottle I had purchased at Harrods the day before.

After the meal, we retired to the East wing, leaving all of the dishes in the dumbwaiter to be dealt with later.

"Noel," I started. "Cyril tells many stories of the perils of the theatre during the war years, and he enjoys telling of the time you gave him your song *Nina (From Argentina)* to perform in a review you were directing. Cyril delights in telling what a beast you were, insisting he sing *Nina* as you sang it. His objection was simply that he was not Noel Coward, and if you wanted it sung like Noel Coward, then perhaps Noel Coward should do it as Noel Coward."

"But of course, dear boy," Noel replied. "You must have talent and be richly gifted to be me! But we did give him full marks for trying."

As I recall some of the conversation that evening, I remember Noel claiming that he often described Cyril as "having a quick wit and a very slow brain." A phrase Cyril was fond of quoting over the years.

As the evening went on, Noel was at the top of his game, as he relished telling the story of Cyril performing *Nina* in his London production of *Sigh No More*. A thought went through my head that made me smile — Cyril will be delighted when I tell him about this evening.

It was late when the gathering ended, and although I may not sing *Nina* to the standard of Noel Coward, I can cook a mean leg of lamb. *Hooray!*

ELIZA'S STEAMED CHOCOLATE PUDDING

4 oz. butter
4 oz. sugar
2 oz. unsweetened chocolate
4 oz. self-rising flour
2 eggs
1 tsp. vanilla
1/2 tsp. salt

4 to 6 Servings

Cream fat and sugar until soft and white. Whisk eggs to a thick froth and gradually beat them into the creamed mixture. Add melted chocolate and vanilla. Lightly stir in flour and salt. Steam 1-1/2 hours. Serve with heavy cream or chocolate sauce or brandy sauce.

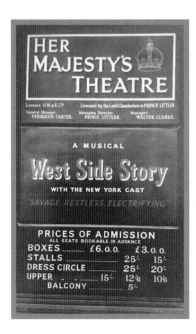

THE PRINCESS

AND

THE PRIME MINISTER

Having royalty in the audience comes with excitement and instructions. Prior to the evening performance, we were called on stage to rehearse the reception of our royal guests after the show. First we were choreographed into lines on stage for the formal reception. As a royal was introduced, we were instructed to bow politely and offer our hand while saying, "Ma'am" or "Sir." Say nothing unless they speak to you, at which time you may answer, but only if spoken to.

We were all lined up on stage as rehearsed. Princess Margaret, younger daughter of King George VI and Queen Elizabeth, could be seen stepping through the wings. She was dressed to the nines in a beautiful pink and green floral dress with a low cut bodice which allowed her diamond neckless to sparkle. She was drop-dead gorgeous. As the procession drew nearer, I could pick up some of the conversations. Protocol went completely out the window. Not one of us adhered to the instructions we were given, all forgetting the curtsy or small gentleman bow, and instead belting out, "How are you?" or "Thank you for coming!" Chita Rivera actually did give a curtsy that went all the way to the ground. We thought she had fallen down.

On another evening, we met Prime Minister Harold McMillan and his wife Lady Dorothy. Since we were not under any instructions in meeting the Prime Minister, we were free to chat. As Lady Dorothy approached me, she dropped her glove. I quickly retrieved it, returning it with a smile. She took the glove without a word and walked on. *How rude,* I thought. A "thank you" would have been polite. Later, I was informed that in England, it's considered bad luck to thank someone for picking up your dropped glove. *Who knew?*

Princess Margaret greeting **West Side Story** *cast members, Eddie Verso (Baby John), Eddie Roll (Action), Sylvia Tysick (Anybodys), George Chakiris (Riff), Ken Leroy (Bernardo)*

71

EDGAR RITCHARD, ARTIST

CYRIL'S YOUNGER BROTHER, Edgar, lived in London. He was an artist with a following. His flat was in Elm Park Gardens in Chelsea. A lovely apartment on the ground floor with tons of light streaming in from Elm Park. The wonderful nine-foot glass doors leading out to the park were the main source of the fantastic light filling his artist's studio.

His living room was his studio, with ten foot ceilings and an electric fireplace with two electric bars. Affluent? I think Edgar thought so; but the heat from the fireplace was adequate only if you were a polar bear.

Cyril commissioned Edgar to do a portrait of me while I was in London. Edgar was a miniature version of Cyril in stature and looks. He was an introvert compared to his big brother. His talent was on canvas. Arriving at Edgar's flat at 10 a.m., he made a cuppa and I sat in a chair on a small platform in the center of the room. Facing me on the wall was a portrait of a young woman. It was Jocelyn Rickards, the very person who replicated the Irene Sharaff costume designs of *West Side Story* for the London production. She had gone through a break-up with English playwright

John Osborne. From the moment I met her, I was madly in love with Jocelyn. It was a happy place to sit, looking at her while having my portrait painted.

By noontime, Edgar put down his brush and announced that it was lunchtime. We went to a small bistro near Sloane Square for lunch. When the check came, I picked it up. *My treat.*

I sat for Edgar two or three times a week and it seemed forever to finish the portrait. It was maddening that on more than one occasion he brushed out the entire work and started over with a sketch. Finally, the day came when he was satisfied with his work; we went to the bistro to celebrate, but this time I ignored the bill when it arrived, obviously indicating to Edgar that he should pay.

"My dear boy," he exclaimed "I was wondering when you would do that!" He continued. "You know, the English have a simple response when it comes to overzealous Americans who generously insist on picking up the tab. We say, 'Oh, thank you!'" (All this being said in an accent that would rival Rex Harrison in *My Fair Lady!*) "A lesson learned dear boy!" Indeed! He paid the tab.

Cyril had Edgar's portrait of me hanging in the apartment at Central Park West until he died in 1977. The painting is now in my office in the basement of my daughter's deli in Clinton Corners getting very, very old, while I…well…Oscar Wilde will tell you.

In the late '60s, Jean and I managed an art exhibition for Edgar at the Qantas Gallery on Fifth Ave, in New York City. As Edgar (and of course Cyril) hailed from Australia, Qantas was eager to give Edgar an exhibition at their Fifth Avenue Gallery. The show was successful and we sold over half the exhibition.

Portrait by Edgar Ritchard, 1959

GEORGE CHAKIRIS (*Riff*)

GEORGE CHAKIRIS played Riff, a Jet, in the London production of *West Side Story*. Great voice and extremely handsome.

This was a great time for me, as George was not only my flat mate, he was my big brother. George is four years my senior and I grew up with three older brothers of whom I was more than just fond. They were there for me and stabilized my life as a kid, and George took their place during this interlude in my extraordinary, ordinary life.

There wasn't anything we didn't do, think, or say without gusto. What an opportunity we were given, being part of a hit show in a magnificent city at an age that allowed us to soak up our surroundings. We took in every historic site and filled our free time with books and talking. *Talking,* does anyone talk anymore? I mean George and I spent hours on subjects that just popped into our heads. I grew up in a Mormon household, George was Greek. Our lives were different, but our values were the same. It was a magic time for me, and I am grateful to have shared this time with George. George and I were both from Los Angeles. His career began in Hollywood films as a dancer. It's impressive, including major roles in *Gentlemen Prefer Blondes, White Christmas, Brigadoon, There's No Business Like Show Business* and many other films.

Our success in the West End of London had its advantages. Most every night there were invitations to parties. George and I would arrive at a party with our West Side Story bags (the ones Pan Am gave us on the flight over). We would have a drink, chat for a few minutes and fill our bag with food and perhaps a bottle of wine, thank the host, and head home to eat. Never invite a dancer to a party if they've just finished a show. They are like a swarm of locusts; within ten minutes, there will be nothing left on the table.

"When You're a Jet, You're a Jet All the Way"
Front row: *Eddie Verso, Riggs O'Hara, Michael Stewart,*
George Chakiris, David Bean, Joe Donovan
Back row: *Tony Mordente, David Holliday,*
Gary Cockrell, Eddie Roll

George has an amazing singing voice. He recorded an album of Gershwin songs, *George on George.* It was fascinating to watch him prepare for the recording sessions. George would sit in a big oversized chair in the flat and silently go over the sheet music note by note. I accompanied him to the recording studio early one morning and observed from the sound booth as George went over the music with the conductor. Minutes later he recorded his first song. He never took off his overcoat. The guy recorded three songs by noon and never removed his coat. He was the same cool brother when he was on stage as *Riff,* leader of the Jets. Cool was his middle name.

George and I often took advantage of the Sundays when our theatre was dark and we had the night off. We sometimes took in a melodrama at a local playhouse. These productions were so much fun, as the audience becomes a willing participant, hissing at the villain and cheering on the heroine.

One evening, during the intermission of one of these melodramas, George and I wandered out to the foyer for tea, as was the custom in English theatres. A rail along the wall provided space for our tea cups and George and I were facing the wall. We turned into the room and found ourselves nose to nose with Rex Harrison and his wife at the time, Kay Kendall. It was quite obvious that they were waiting for us to turn around so they could speak to us. Acknowledging the intrusion of our space, they quickly apologized, but wanted to let us know how much they enjoyed seeing *West Side Story*. We talked for a few minutes until the house lights dimmed, signaling that the second act was about to begin. With his towering frame, Rex was very imposing, while Kay was happily chatting us up, and full of life.

CHITA RIVERA
(Anita)

IT'S ABOUT JOY, it's about living, it's about music and dance. This is Chita. She is the epitome of our family's 180 Rule. Jerry Robbins loved her because of this. Even in rehearsals she never marked a step.

We first met during rehearsals at the Alvin Theatre in New York City. She was a brilliant star from the get-go. Everything about her was exciting. She lit up the room, already filled with the sound of her voice, exuding her positive lifestyle. On stage she was no different. Her moves were confident, exact, always in perfect control. Watching her do *America* from the wings was an honor.

Tony Mordente and Chita were married during the New York run of *West Side Story* in 1957. Tony was one of the original Jets *(A-Rab)*

76

in the original Broadway and London productions. He played the role of *Action* in the
1961 film version. Tony was one helluva
dancer. Like Chita, he was explosive. Before each show, the cast was required to be
on stage "one half hour before 'Half Hour'"
for a jazz-ballet warm-up class! This often
led to a challenge with the dancers and involved showing off with triple tours (three
turns in the air) and fun, difficult dance
combinations. The kids excelled in these
challenges.

Chita's career started out like most
dancers — slogging your guts out every day
in classes and hoping against huge odds that
something will come your way. What did
come her way, and what she has accom-

"America"

plished in her career has been so deserving: two Tony Awards, eight
Tony nominations. The Kennedy Center Honors Award, and the
Presidential Medal of Freedom Award given to her by President Obama.
She is still "treading the boards" (performing on stage) and going strong.
Cheers, Chita!

Tony and Chita lived in a London townhouse with lots of room to
host their continual flow of friends and family. Every Saturday night Tony
hosted a poker game that played on till early Sunday morning. I don't
think I missed a game — even though I never played. I simply observed.
The food was abundant and Chita made you feel so warmly welcomed.
It felt like being home, especially for an 18-year-old kid who was living
an extraordinary life in an extraordinary show, thousands of miles from
his family.

DAVID HOLLIDAY

D AVID HOLLIDAY was straight out of college—tall, blond, handsome and very quiet. On our five-minute breaks during early rehearsals at the Alvin Theatre, I would often sit and chat with him. This was the beginning of a lifelong friendship.

Since the *West Side Story* role of *Gladhand* (the social worker in the Dance Hall scene) required no singing, one only thought of David as a good actor. When he was given the part, he actually didn't think of himself as a singer. As *Gladhand*, he was wonderful. But little did anyone know of the talent in both acting and singing that would emerge from this kid.

A graduate of Carthage College, Wisconsin, David studied seriously and developed a beautiful voice which would serve him well. He understudied *Tony* in the show and eventually took over the role. His passion and love of the theatre arts was beyond words. It was exciting to watch him develop and become a star. In 1961, David played *Tony* for the entire year with Jean and me in the British tour of *West Side Story*.

David's break came in 1962 when Noel Coward signed him for a starring role with Elaine Stritch in *Sail Away* at the Savoy Theatre in London.

He did a fantastic job playing Frank Butler in *Annie Get Your Gun* in Copenhagen, singing the entire score phonetically in Danish. David went on to win the Theater World Award in New York for his performance in *Coco* with Katharine Hepburn. Jean and I once drove up to Rochester, New York to see David playing as Don Quixote in *Man of La Mancha*.

For most of his 30-year career, David lived on the 40th floor of the government-subsidized Manhattan Towers on 43rd and Tenth Avenue in New York City. Built for people of the theatre world, the Towers offered housing for stagehands, opera singers, make-up artists, songwriters. It didn't matter — as long as you were in the theatre business in one capacity or another. David's was our go-to-place when we were in NYC.

LIONEL BART, SONGWRITER/PRODUCER

HER MAJESTY'S THEATRE, at the bottom of the Haymarket, was a melting pot of theatre people — actors, dancers, and writers that hung out with the cast members. We befriended Lionel Bart. He had written a couple of rock-and-roll hits for Tommy Steele, who was the British answer to Elvis Presley in the late 1950s. A few of us were invited back to his mews flat to sing a new libretto he had just written. The taxi left us off at the end of the mews and we walked the cobblestones to #6.

Entering the flat, you knew immediately that this chap had had success somewhere along the way. The flat had central heating, whereas the norm in most British homes was to have a single electric bar in each room. We settled in and opened a bottle of wine. Lionel passed out the librettos and sitting around the piano he accompanied us singing the entire score of *Oliver*. It was brilliant. I mean the libretto, not us. We stunk. Laughter filled the room as we encouraged Lionel on.

Lionel Bart went on to produce *Oliver* in NYC in 1960, winning a Tony Award for Best Musical.

Other shows that Lionel wrote with moderate success were *Things Ain't What They Used To Be, Lock Up Your Daughters,* and in 1962 *Blitz.* (Cyril appeared in a production of *Lock Up Your Daughters* in NYC.)

Jean and I saw *Blitz* (about World War II and the blitz of London). It was still a stinging memory to most Brits in the '50s. Surely anyone having been part of The Blitz didn't want a reminder. The show was a bomb, no pun intended.

Lionel had written two other musicals, *Twang* and *La Strada.* and he was very passionate about producing them. So he decided to sell the rights to *Oliver* to finance it. This decision cost him millions. He ended up selling *Oliver* for £350 ($1,000) to Max Bygraves, a popular English actor-comedian-singer, who later, it is reported, sold the rights for nearly one million dollars.

OUT AND ABOUT IN LONDON

Singing Lessons

I TOOK SINGING LESSONS with a Welsh tenor — a Welshman who loved to sing *your* lesson, accompanied on the piano by Mrs. Brrrrown. While coaching us, our Welsh tenor would place the thumb of his right hand on the edge of his upper teeth. With his left hand, in a circular motion in front of his face, he would make resonant noises coming from his sinus or nasal passage . . . as if this motion would encourage us to *"Project, project!"*

Several of the kids in the company were studying with him. Every night before the curtain went up, you could hear us practice our notes, pressing our thumb to our upper teeth and waving our hand around in front of our faces so as to encourage a resounding noise from our diaphragm and through our head cavity. It wasn't until much later that we discovered our Welsh tenor was not asking us to project; he was actually holding on to his upper plate with the thumb of his right hand. We don't know why he made circles in the air with his left hand.

The Royal Festival Hall

I WAS 18 YEARS OLD, working in London and thought of myself as rather worldly. I mean, my career was on a roll and I was working in another hit show — in London no less. It had never occurred to me that I hadn't experienced everything life had to offer. Monday through Saturday we performed eight shows, including matinee performances on Wednesday and Saturday. Sunday, our theatre was dark and we enjoyed a well-deserved day off.

One particular Sunday, I was lounging around having my morning tea. *You see that? I was having tea. How sophisticated and worldly!* The telephone rang. It was Sarah and Jeremy Grayson, the couple we had "kidnapped" in Piccadilly Circus on our opening night.

"What are you doing this evening?" Sarah asked. "Have you any plans? Jeremy and I were wondering if you'd like to join us?"

They had tickets for the Royal Festival Hall to take in a concert. The London Philharmonic was performing a Tchaikovsky program. I had never been to the Festival Hall.

It was at that moment that I realized just how unsophisticated I really was. I had never actually heard a live orchestra in concert. In fact, I had never even been to *any* concert. But I did have a collection of classical LPs and was a huge fan of classical music. Mother was a classical pianist and we grew up on the classical music emanating from the upright piano in our living room. Cyril had an enormous influence, introducing me to operas and a wide range of classical music. But this would be a first for me. I accepted their invitation without hesitation. Before Sarah hung up, we agreed to meet at the Festival Hall before the concert.

As the taxi drove across Waterloo Bridge to the south side of the Thames, I had a picture-perfect view of the Royal Festival Hall lit in a spectacular glow on the bank of the River. Meeting the Graysons as planned, we made our way into the massive Hall to find our seats. Patiently we waited as the Hall began to fill around us. The buzz of the audience moving about, looking for their seats, was blending with the

80-piece orchestra moving about and tuning their instruments. The atmosphere was exhilarating. There I was, sitting with my new friends in a new environment, uncertain of what I was about to experience. Then the lights dimmed and the conductor walked out to the podium to polite applause.

Turning to face the audience, he raised both arms, instructing the audience to rise. For the first time, I heard the sound of a thousand people rising in unison.

Satisfied that the entire audience was on their feet, the conductor turned back to the orchestra, tapped the podium with his baton, and gave a downbeat — to a moment that will live in my soul forever. This magnificent orchestra played *God Save The Queen.* I thought I had died and ascended to heaven. There wasn't a part of me that wasn't covered in goosebumps. Never had I heard anything so powerful and beautiful. I was speechless; and this was only the start of the evening.

The program included Tchaikovsky's *Violin Concerto in D major.* As the sound of the orchestra's music filled the Hall with this brilliant masterpiece, it profoundly touched me to the core of my soul. I was a limp rag by the end of the night. That magnificent concerto has been my all-time favorite piece of music ever since. I own several versions by various artists, from David Oistrakh, Itzhak Perlman, Yehudi Menuhin, and Joshua Bell, and Nigel Kennedy from London.

Gala Performances

BEING PART OF A HIT SHOW had its perks. Benefit gala performances given for charitable functions were assembled from current hit shows performing in the West End. *West Side Story* was one of those shows asked to perform for many such events. There could be several shows asked to participate in the evening, usually performing only one number from each show, making for an exciting evening.

The London Palladium was the site for a Royal Gala attended by the Queen and Prince Phillip. This particular evening we were asked to perform *Gee, Officer Krupke.* In the song, I played *Officer Krupke,* whacking the guys on the head with a rolled-up newspaper for which they sang the song *Gee, Officer Krupke* to me. (I did the same part in the movie version.) Danny Kaye hosted the evening and conducted the Royal Philharmonic Orchestra. It was a spoof whereby Mr. Kaye broke several batons and fell off the podium often to peals of laughter from an adoring audience.

At another gala at the Drury Lane Theatre, we performed the dance number *Cool.* The Georgian National Ballet was on the bill that evening. During rehearsals, we exchanged dance techniques, mostly knee turns and fantastic spins they did as second nature. We, on the other hand, nearly killed ourselves. The encounter was even more astounding as we neither spoke each other's language. But we became friends during the rehearsals. With the utmost respect, our *West Side Story* dancers agreed that a career with the Georgian National Ballet would be a short one for any of us — total knee failure was a certainty!

Margot Fonteyn and Michael Somes performed a duet from the ballet *Giselle.* Ms. Fonteyn was amazing. Being on the board of directors of the Royal Academy of Dance, she had asked a few of us dancers from *West Side Story* to give exhibitions for the Academy. It was interesting that these British dancers were never taught the dynamics of dance. However perfect their dance technique may have been, an inner soul was lacking. We also found this with the replacement dancers in our show. As the Americans left the show, they were replaced by Brits. Until we arrived on the scene, the Brits were not taught to dance from the inside out, with emotion. In the end, we were credited with bringing a new era of dance to Britain in the late '50s.

Today, British dancers are in the mix and can dance on a level with anyone on the planet. Jerome Robbins had a lot to do with that. His Ballet USA is a perfect example of beautiful jazz-ballet with unbelievable emotion and style. Jerry choreographed in the method actors fashion. His movement spoke to you. Every dance combination was scripted — every movement said something.

With Eddie Verso in Switzerland, 1960

TWO JETS ON A TOUR OF EUROPE

EDDIE VERSO was the youngest of the cast. As *Baby John,* he fit the part — skinny, young, and a beautiful dancer. Ballet was his forte. Eddie was with Jerry Robbins' Ballet USA as well as the New York City Ballet Company. We both decided to leave the London Company of *West Side Story* and pop over to Europe before returning to New York. We actually drove the Wolseley onto a tiny eight-seater airplane that flew us to Belgium.

Our six-week trip through Europe began without an itinerary. We had maps and a lot of guts. We stocked up on gas coupons and joined the Youth Hostel Association! For five dollars each, we belonged to a non-profit group that maintained housing facilities all over the world. For a nominal fee, you got a bed, shower, breakfast, and sometimes dinner.

As you arrived, you signed up for a job. It might be mopping floors, or washing dishes, or anything else to help out, as the staff was all voluntary. The men slept separately from the women, even if you were a married couple. The concept is quite wonderful and a great opportunity to meet people from all over the world. Although it was called a "Youth Hostel," most of the patrons we met were adults.

For a month and a half, we toured Europe. Returning to London was a nice feeling. It felt like home. We were there a short time when Eddie received a call from Jerry Robbins directing him to make his way to Hollywood to test for the film

Leaning on my 1959 Wolseley 1500

version of *West Side Story*. It was very exciting and we threw a goodbye party for Eddie that ended at Heathrow Airport. Joined by others from the London show, Jean Deeks and I saw him off with great fanfare. I stayed another two weeks in London with Jean and then booked a slow boat back to New York.

In order to get one board the *SS United States*, I took a train to Southampton and, to my surprise, David Holliday drove Jean down to the docks in his '59 MGA. I was already boarded and was standing at the bow of the ship all alone when I saw them drive up to the dock. Jean jumped out of the car and was frantically waving as the ship slowly backed out of its slip. I stood there waving until they were out of sight. I had never felt so alone in all my life.

Jean Deeks

~ 5 ~

Enter
Miss Jean Deeks

I N THE SUMMER OF 1959, Jean Deeks joined the London company of *West Side Story*. She had never seen the show prior to her audition and had no idea what to expect. Tony Mordente, dance captain for the company, was giving the audition on stage at Her Majesty's Theatre where we played eight shows a week.

Tony was looking for a dancer who could swing the show (covering all the dance routines of the girls in the show), and also understudy *Anybodys,* the tomboy in *West Side Story* who desperately wanted to be a member of the Jets. By the summer of '59, some of the dancers were leaving the show. We were an all-American cast and British Equity allowed for this arrangement; but replacements had to be British.

The auditions were underway, when out popped this beautiful five-foot tall redhead. But beauty was not Tony's top priority. Passion with guts was what he was trying to get from the dancers.

"You!" He pointed to the redhead.

"What's your name?"

"Jean Deeks," she replied, with confidence.

"Well, Jean Deeks, auditions for *West Side Story* are not usually given in point shoes."

As we now know, Jean had no idea what *West Side Story* was about prior to the audition. Tony liked her, offered her the job of *Swing Girl* and understudy to *Anybodys*. Although it took over four months for Jean and I to get acquainted, I was the ultimate winner.

Eddie Roll was the original *Action* in the Broadway production of *West Wide Story*. He and his wife, Inga, were both performing in the London production. Inga was my dance partner in the *Dance at the Gym*. As fate would have it, she and Eddie became expectant parents and Jean Deeks was to be her replacement, dancing with me in the *Dance at the Gym*. Jean Deeks was drop-dead gorgeous. Except for rehearsals, I didn't really get to know her. Time came for Inga to leave the show and Jean took her place as my partner. The very first night in the dance hall, Jean found herself in the wrong place and I tripped over her spraining my ankle.

Between the first and second act, Eddie Roll and I would meet in the basement under the stage, where for thrupence, Jimmy (a stage-hand) would make us a "cuppa" lovely tea. We sat on a long wooden bench and carried on a conversation in character, a la method acting. (You can still be a method actor and drink a cup of tea in character.) Eddie always arrived a couple of minutes late and at the end of the bench sat this beautiful Jean Deeks. Our conversation was brief and the same every night.

"Hi, gorgeous, what about a date Friday night?"

"Na," she would retort, "How about Saturday?"

"Too bad, I'm busy!"

Eddie would appear at this moment and sit between us, thus cutting off our prattle. This went on for weeks. One night Eddie didn't show up to stop the prattle and we were sort of dumbfounded sitting there looking at each other. Eventually I broke the silence. "I'm not doing anything really. Sunday I'm spending the day cleaning the house! Not too exciting!" Jean paused a minute then simply said, "Tell you what, mate. You leave the key under the mat and I'll wake you with a cuppa." I did, she did and my oh my... that was sixty-two years ago.

There is a footnote to this story. Jean helped me with the cleaning and I cooked dinner for her and then drove her home. *Yep!* That's a true story. A gentleman all the way. I even met her Mum and Dad that evening. That was in the fall of 1959 and our initial courtship was relatively short.

***Jean Deeks entertaining American troops
in Germany at the age of 17***

GROWING UP IN ENGLAND

AS AN ENERGETIC YOUNG DANCING GIRL IN ENGLAND, Jean Deeks established a stellar background when her mother sent her off to Kathleen Mumford's School of Ballet. Her mother's reason? Simply to prevent the linoleum flooring in their home from wearing out. Or, in her Mum's words, *"Ere mate, yer not wearin' out my flooring with all yer dancin' about!"* That was her mother's lament, in a genuine Cockney accent.

And so it was — her own fairy tale came true — Jean's career blossomed. At age 11, she entered and won a prestigious scholarship to the Royal Academy of Dance. There was no doubt her career path was in the Arts.

The local paper proclaimed:

Young Dancer with Ability

Young Jean Deeks of Greenford, Middlesex, a student at the Royal Academy of Dancing, has just won a fourth-year scholarship. Scholarship students are "weeded out" every year, and to win a fourth year award is "really something."

Jean, who won a cup for her character dancing at the recent Ealing Festival, showed visitors to the senior concert that she is possessed of remarkable ability for her age.

At the Royal Academy, Jean earned all the essential teaching degrees required for teaching dance in Great Britain. Her certificates and medals complete one entire scrapbook in our library at home. Many of these certificates are adjudicated and signed by the aforementioned Margot

Fonteyn as well as by Pamela May, British dancers and teachers of classical ballet.

By age twelve, Jean was dancing in British Theatre productions of Enid Blyton's *Noddy in Toyland* at the Stoll Theatre in London. Dancing in numerous television specials, she was indeed "the working girl." Jean was a back-up dancer with the popular Ernest Maxim's TV shows, dancing with guest stars Harry Belafonte, Eddie Fisher, Petula Clark, and Adam Faith. She toured with popular pantomime productions of *Jack and the Beanstalk* and *Cinderella.* By age seventeen, she entertained the American Army troops in Germany, dancing for the American choreographer Norman Walker.

Jean's father, Ernie, was not much taller than his daughter. He worked at the BBC. Jean was never shy to brag that her father worked at the BBC, when asked by the upper-class students at the Royal Academy. Impressive? Certainly, but she never told them that the acronym BBC was the British Bath Company, not British Broadcasting Company. The British Bath Company was a massive plant that produced porcelain bath tubs and toilets. Ernie's job was to keep the plant running. When a machine broke down, he got it back on line, even if it required making the broken part. The plant was located directly behind their home. Dad had only to jump the fence to go to work.

Every Tuesday, the Bath Company fired up their blast furnace and melted down scrap metal. The process required a flux process that gave off an acrid smell in the neighborhood. Directly across the rail tracks was Lyons Tea Co. which roasted coffee on Thursdays. One always knew whether it was Tuesday or Thursday without asking.

Mum was the cook and gardener. She took loving care of the garden, changing it 'round every year. Fish pond this year, greenhouse the next. A born Cockney, she dropped 'er Hs properly, making it difficult to understand a word of what she said.

As Jean was now firmly ensconced at the Royal Academy, her mother was hellbent on having her speak proper English. Off to elocution

Jean, me, Gran Membery, Dorothy Deeks on the River Thames, 1961

classes Jean went—so as not to talk like 'er. "Now you speak proper," she would demand of her daughter. "No girl of mine should talk like me at the posh Royal Academy."

Gran Membery lived in St. Peter's Cottage on the River Thames in Hammersmith. The day we were to meet her, I was instructed to knock at the door and ask for "Gran." The door opened and I truly thought the woman standing in front of me was the charlady ready to clean the house.

"Would Gran Membery be home?" I asked. This tiny ball of a woman, who I truly thought was the help, threw open her arms and declared, "I'm yer Nan, matey! Give us a kiss then!" With a tooth missing, her smile was welcoming and I knew instantly we would be the best of mates.

St. Peter's Cottage was on the East side of the Thames and just south of the Hammersmith Bridge. From her backyard, we had a perfect view of the University Boat Race, featuring Cambridge and Oxford. The family always boasted to me that St. Peter's Cottage was next door to A.P. Herbert. "Really?" I would respond — careful not to let on that I was clueless about A.P. Herbert. (Alan Patrick Herbert was an acclaimed author and member of Parliament from 1935-1950.)

Nan's kitchen door led to the garden and out to the Thames. Most important, it also led you to the two-seater just outside the kitchen door. I couldn't imagine living there in the winter, having to leave the house to use the toilet. God only knows where Gran purchased her toilet paper. It came with a wax coating and if you held it up to the light one could read the watermark, "Property of the UK!" Royalty? It was a royal pain and quite useless, with its waxy finish.

Jean tells many stories of standing on the stone wall at the bottom of Nan's garden, being held by granddad Membery during The Blitz in the early '40s. Mum refused to evacuate Jean during the war.

"If I go, me ole love, we all go!" But they still ran to the coal hole for shelter or to the underground tube station where, to her delight, they ate "bread and drippin'" with the muffled sound of the bombing echoed through the tube station.

Heading north from St. Peter's Cottage was the Black Lion, a classic English Pub where you might find one of us having a pint. On our block was a beautiful park boasting a bronze statue of a naked man without a fig leaf. I'm sure it's the same park used in the film, *Notting Hill,* starring Julia Roberts and Hugh Grant, where the couple spots a dedication on a park bench:

> *For June, who loved this garden*
> *From Joseph, who always sat beside her.*

SAVING OUR MEMORIES

THEY SAY THAT OPPOSITES ATTRACT. Jean and I represent the perfect example. I have a compulsive habit of documenting most every event of our lives. Every January we begin with a new scrapbook, an annual tradition I started in the mid-'50s. We chronicle nearly every month of our lives. Unfortunately, we have no memorabilia from Jean's life prior to her joining *West Side Story* in 1959.

At twelve years old, Jean commuted from Greenford to London by tube, performing at the Royal Festival Hall in *Where the Rainbow Ends* with Anton Dolin and Alicia Markova. Regrettably, there are no *Playbills,* programs, news articles, or reviews of any West End pantomimes she danced in. Apart from the memories, the details are lost.

Then she met me, a cataloger of life. We ended up building a special bookcase in the study of our home just to house the scrapbooks. When Jean's parents passed, we received a box of family documents that made a beautiful family history dating back to Jean's grandparents and World War I. Sadly, no memorabilia of her early theatre life were in the treasure box.

"Tiger" in the original West Side Story *movie*

~ 6 ~

West Side Story (1961 Movie)

SAMUEL GOLDWYN STUDIO

(HOLLYWOOD)

Here I was back in New York again! Arriving in the port of New York is indeed an experience to savor. Just passing the "Lady" is powerful. It's an impressive sight and a memorable feeling of pride to have her standing in the harbor to welcome you home.

I booked a flight to Los Angeles to visit my family. I had been away for 18 months and was looking forward to being in LA again. Before leaving, I called my agent, Milton Goldman. He had a memo from Jerry Robbins and a request for me to be in Hollywood ASAP for a screen test for the film version of *West Side Story.* "Wear rehearsal clothes" was a postscript on Jerry's memo. *Perfect, I was on my way.*

The portals at the gate loomed large approaching the movie lot of Samuel Goldwyn Studio off Santa Monica Boulevard in West Hollywood.

This is it, I thought to myself. I couldn't believe I was here, about to drive onto a movie studio lot. Here I was living a fantasy that I had dreamed about since I was eight years old. I pulled up to the gate, gave the chap my name and was directed to the gym where I quickly changed into rehearsal clothes and joined other dancers. It was old home week again. I had already worked with some of the dancers present: Tony Mordente, Howard Jeffrey, Tommy Abbott, Eddie Verso, Jay Norman, and Bobby Thompson. With Betty Walberg at the piano, Howard Jeffrey gave us a warm-up class. I felt great!

Jerry Robbins arrived with great fanfare. There it was, Jerry's distinctive giggle-laugh. I knew I was in the right place. As Jerry focused on the *Prologue,* we worked on various dance sections, while he created what seemed like sixteen different ways to dance every eight bars of music. He was serious, but fun, all at the same time. In the end, we didn't keep much of the new choreography.

The film version was a slight variation of the original Broadway show. The number *America* would eventually be rechoreographed when Robbins added the Shark Boys to the dance number. The original Broadway production of *America* only involved the Shark Girls, with Chita Rivera, which was a show stopper. Adding George Chakiris and the Shark Boys, doubled the excitement. I was a Jet, and wasn't involved in that number.

Most of the cast had already performed in a *West Side Story* stage version and so the pressure that normally comes with new choreography was not there. Jerry was easy and relaxed most of the time, with me anyway. Actually, time had mellowed Jerry. He was quite wonderful to work with during the filming.

I never did a formal screen test. One afternoon three of us (Tony Mordente, David Winters and I), were summoned to Studio B on the lot where we were instructed to be gang members on camera. Jerry and Robert Wise, the co-directors, were sitting off-camera throwing questions at us and anything they could think of to get us to react. All of this on

Jets in The PROLOGUE

l. to r. : Russ Tamblyn, Tucker Smith, Tony Mordente, David Winters, me, Harvey Evans, Eliot Feld (kneeling)

The PROLOGUE: FIRST ENCOUNTER WITH A SHARK

George Chakiris (as Bernardo, a Shark); David Bean (as Tiger, a Jet); Tucker Smith (as Ice, a Jet)

"When you're a Jet, you're the swingin'est thing:
Little boy, you're a man; little man, you're a king!"

BIG DEAL	TIGER	MOUTHPIECE
Scooter Teague	*David Bean*	*Harvey Evans*
ICE	GEE–TAR	BABY JOHN
Tucker Smith	*Tommy Abbott*	*Eliot Feld*
JOY BOY	SNOWBOY	ACTION
Bobby Banas	*Bert Michaels*	*Tony Mordente*
A–RAB		
David Winters		

98

camera. We spent a couple of hours improvising with the two of them. Later I was told they were testing 70 mm film used for the end product. This was as close to a screen test as I can remember.

All this time, my red hair was growing longer and longer — again! It was actually hitting my shoulders, and Jerry enjoyed calling me "Tiger." I just may have looked like a tiger.

On a very hot afternoon, the Jets were called together on the pavement outside one of the studios. We formed a circle around Jerry, Robert Wise, and Assistant Director, Bob Relyea. As they walked around the inner circle of Jets, each one of us was asked to turn our backs. As I turned I heard Jerry say, *"him."* Within an hour, I had been given a crewcut. It reminded me of the time Mary Martin and Perry Como cut my hair. Nevertheless, my name stayed; I continued to be *Tiger* in the movie.

From day one, the acclaimed composer and musical director Saul Chaplin was always at our rehearsals. I didn't know who he was or what he had done. He was tall, with grayish hair and a wonky eye. You never quite knew if he was talking to you or the person next to you. I had no clue who I was working with — there was no Google in those days. This man was awarded three Academy Awards in music scoring: *American in Paris, Seven Brides for Seven Brothers,* and ultimately our *West Side Story*.

Chaplin also went on to win an Academy Award as co-producer of the *Sound of Music.* His body of work is amazing. Back in the '30s, his music career included working with Sammy Cahn and writing hits for such greats as The Andrews Sisters.

Saul was given the job of working with Tucker Smith *(Ice)* and me *(Tiger)* on the *Jet Song.* Robbins and Wise were not happy with Russ Tamblyn's sound track of the song, so we were asked to record it as a possible replacement.

I worked with Saul for a couple of days, belting out the song while he played on the piano, stopping me at intervals with instructions.

"Don't get lyrical, David," Saul said. "They want you to sound like Russ."

JERRY AND THE JETS (plus one Shark)

Jerry and Bob were called in to hear the playbacks. As my version of the song ended, I heard Jerry say, "David sounds just like Russ!" followed by his signature laugh. They went with Tucker. His voice is the one you hear on the sound track singing the *Jet Song*. Russ Tamblyn did not sing it for the final cut in the film, although I personally thought the Tamblyn version was equal to Tucker's.

Photo at right: FILMING THE PROLOGUE
Dancers (l. to r.): Me, Bert Michaels, Harvey Evans, Tucker Smith, Eliot Feld
On the boom: Jerry Robbins and Daniel Fapp (cinematographer)

FILMING IN N.Y.C.

W E ARRIVED IN NYC in June of 1960 as the summer was in bloom and the weather allowed us to dance in the streets. The cast was booked into the Wyndham Hotel on 56th Street. A bus would greet us in the morning just outside the hotel and transport all of us to the 110th Street school playground on the Upper East Side, or 66th Street on the West Side. Our personal belongings stayed on the bus during the day, as the bus was our go-to place if it rained or if anyone needed a nap. More often, it was our "jail" when we were naughty.

Our day started with a 6 a.m. makeup call in the hotel. Costume call was next and then the bus trip. Every morning on the film site, Jerry would give us a ballet barre right on the sidewalk. Must have been a sight; all these hoodlum-looking dudes on the street, moving their arms and legs, doing point tondu and grand plies with an appropriate *port de bra.*

Warm-up was mandatory to prevent injury, especially as we were dancing on the street. Robert Wise and Jerry worked very closely on the *Prologue*, which was filmed entirely in NYC. They both were constantly

viewing every move we made through their small viewfinders that hung from their necks. If we were in a dance sequence, we rehearsed every second of the shot until we did a take. Sometimes only a take or two and it was in the can. Other times we did ten or fifteen takes because Jerry was a perfectionist and had us do take after take, while Bob patiently sat on the boom and waited. A loud horn or a truck traveling by would stop the shoot.

The process of breaking down a set-up and getting ready for the next shot took time. Time of which the Jets and Sharks could find ways to get relegated to the bus.

Our funniest "extracurricular activity" was our famous *Rain Dance*. For no real reason, we choreographed an "Indian-style" rain dance that proved entertaining to the crowds and crew watching on the street. The powers that be on set didn't enjoy it—simply because it seemed that we were magic. Every time we danced the *Rain Dance* — you guessed it — *it rained!*

This was an economic disaster for the Mirisch brothers (our producers), and we were being blamed for the delay. *Go to jail! Go directly to jail. Do not pass Go. Back to the bus.*

The company had a bigger problem on the Upper East Side. Shooting in the playground on 110th Street was drawing a lot of attention. People living in the apartments would hang out of their windows to watch all of us dancing. They could be seen in most of the shots. The only solution was to pay them off, which the company did — handsomely. Our other problem was the actual gangs that ruled the streets on the Upper East Side. These gangs felt invaded and the smartest thing the company did was to hire them for protection. They even shared our bus. *Absolutely brilliant!*

These gang members became part of the crew and hung out with us. They couldn't believe we were so tough and then when the music playback started, we all sprang into action singing and dancing on the sidewalk, *When you're a Jet, you're a Jet all the way.* It blew them away.

Many stories have floated around, depicting odd and sometimes funny circumstances during the filming of *West Side Story,* both in

Hollywood and New York. One such story happened on a summer day in the City, involving co-directors Robert and Jerry. They were shooting a dance scene in the street, and it was hot as hell.

The co-directors agreed on the location for the shoot and the rehearsals went without problems. When the decision was made to shoot, the speakers spewed out the music and the dancers went through the choreography without a flaw. Bob looked at Jerry and said, "Looks good to me." But Robbins wanted to shoot one more. Then another, and another.

Wise finally insisted, "That's a wrap." At that point, Robbins gathered the dancers together and, legend has it, he declared, "We'll do this one more time, only this time do the whole thing on your left foot."

It's a great story, but it never happened. Jerry may have said this as a joke, but think about it. It would take three days of rehearsals to flip-flop even a few bars from one foot to the other.

At the time of our filming, the buildings on 61st through 68th Streets were being demolished to make way for the new Lincoln Center. When you watch the 1961 *West Side Story* movie, you'll see us chase a Shark into a building during the *Prologue*. But there isn't anything beyond that front door. All the front parts of the buildings were spared for the film. As soon as we departed, they demolished the rest of the buildings and built the Center.

COMPETITION: JETS VS. SHARKS

IN THE HEAT OF THE SUMMER, Jerry had finished the choreography for *Cool*. We rehearsed every day in the blistering heat without Jerry while he rechoreographed *America,* adding the Shark boys to the number. Jerry continued the tension between the two gangs by having the Sharks, with George Chakiris and Rita Moreno, do a complete run through of *America* in the studio. Everybody on the lot was invited and the studio was packed. When the Sharks finished the dance, the room exploded. *Very exciting!*

Immediately following this, the Jets had to take the floor and do *Cool*. Jerry had choreographed all the musical numbers as a complete continuous piece. When we filmed each number, it was broken up into eight or sixteen bar segments; but for run-throughs, we did the entire dance number. *Cool* created tension that filled the studio. At the end of the number, there was dead silence. The contrast in the studio between the Jets and Sharks was a tool Jerry used every chance he could. It worked.

NATALIE WOOD *(Maria)*

WHEN SHE WAS AT THE STUDIO, Natalie joined us every morning for class in the gym. If we were shooting on the set, we went straight to make-up. If we were not on call, we had class in the gym. She didn't stay for the full class, it being slightly beyond her ability. That class was way above most dancers' ability. Halfway through the class, we used to sit it out and just watch Tony Mordente, Eddie Verso, Tommy Abbott and Jay Norman get challenged by Jerry with dance combinations that were virtually impossible... beautiful to watch but very difficult to do.

No one left the gym. We all hung around to watch. One morning, I was sitting next to Natalie and she turned to say something to me. As I turned to look at her, I remember losing my breath; she was that beautiful!

The Jets didn't have much to do with Natalie on screen — only the Dance Hall scene at the beginning of the film, and when they carried Tony away, at the very end of the film. That was it for most of us. Remember, Jerry kept the Jets and Sharks apart. No mingling. Taking class in the mornings was the exception. But that was early on during early development; and most of Natalie's scenes were filmed on a closed set. Although she was on the Studio lot, we didn't technically work with her all that much.

Natalie Wood

Natalie was very much the go-to girl. If any of the cast members needed anything, we went to her first; all it took was one word from her and we had it.

From the beginning, Natalie was under the impression she would do all her own singing. She worked hard with Saul Chaplin, who assisted the musical director, Johnny Green. In rehearsals, it was her voice you heard on the playback. Marni Nixon, who was a ghost singer for many actresses, was brought in to record the voice of Maria. She even recorded some of Rita Moreno's vocals. Without a doubt, she was a talent and did a wonderful job; but that's not to say that Natalie wasn't upset at being misled about not using her own voice for the final score.

She was married to Robert Wagner who hung out on the lot whenever Natalie was working. Everyone called him "R.J." There is a lot of hanging around while making a movie, and it was normal to pop into the commissary and plop down next to a celeb as though you had been doing this all your life.

RUSS TAMBLYN *(Riff)*

IT WAS SUMMER and time was flying by. Russ bought a new Mercedes 120 SL, one of those sporty convertibles. A test drive was mandatory and we found ourselves flying through the streets of Hollywood with the top down, sitting on top of the back seat singing at the top of our lungs.

Russ was fun. His positive approach made it a joy to greet the day. Although Russ and I couldn't be more American, we did have one foreign interest in common. Russ was dating a Brit named Elizabeth and I was spending a fortune with Ma Bell talking with Jean in London. We were in the studio filming the *Tonight Quintet* when I was summoned to the main office for an important phone call. Who in the world would call me at the studio?

I rushed to the office to be greeted on the telephone by a rep of the phone company demanding that I pay my telephone bill. It seems Jean and I were on the phone more than was comfortable for the phone company and our last chat amounted to hundreds of dollars. This call raised a red flag with the company. Would I please come to their office in Hollywood and pay the bill? At the time, I was in full makeup and not about to run off to make Ma Bell happy. After all, my bill wasn't delinquent, just a little over the mark; I put the blame on long-distance hormonal imbalance. Russ was going through the same illness, though not as long-distance, as his British mate resided in Hollywood.

Russ did marry Elizabeth Kempton in 1960 and they had a baby girl named China. In 1981, Russ remarried and he and his new bride Bonnie welcomed their baby girl Amber into the world in 1983. A beautiful young actress who is very talented and successful in her own right.

Russ was not a dancer's dancer. As he himself often acknowledges, he was a "great tumbler" and, I would add, he moved beautifully. Jerry Robbins never had a problem with Russ, a seasoned professional with an impressive history. *Seven Brides for Seven Brothers* comes to mind.

"THAT'S A TOUCHIN' GOOD STORY..."
from "Gee, Officer Krupke"

Me, Bert Michaels, and Russ Tamblyn

GEE, OFFICER KRUPKE

"GEE, OFFICER KRUPKE," one of the most popular songs in *West Side Story,* was written by Stephen Sondheim, with music by Leonard Bernstein. I was thrilled to be chosen to play the part of Officer Krupke in the song — both in the 1958 London production and in the original 1961 film.

I start the song on the sidewalk outside of Doc's Drugstore by mocking Officer Krupke as he drove off responding to an emergency call. Smacking my brother Jets on the head with rolled up newspaper was great fun!

"Give me one good reason for not draggin' ya down to the station house ya punks!" *Whack!*

When I got around to whacking Riff, played by Russ, he dropped to his knees and started singing the line, "Dear kindly Sergeant Krupke." Russ led the song with a few others having solo parts — the headshrinker, the social worker, and the judge. All of our little asides and chatter were spontaneous and were kept in as part of the song. This really made our performance feel as though we were making it all up on the spot as we went along!

RITA MORENO (*Anita*)

THE MOST FLATTERING THING anyone can say about Rita: she is the ultimate pro. There isn't anything she hasn't done in the business that hasn't been 180%. This woman explodes with confidence and energy in every breath she takes. You can't help being up when in her company.

Her career has been beyond fantastic for the past seven decades. Working with her was a joy and a pleasure. She has been a strong member of the gang that makes up the 60-year-old cast of *West Side Story* from Hollywood. Rita is an "E.G.O.T.," which translates as a winner of an Emmy, a Grammy, an Oscar, and a Tony award. One of only sixteen people to have received the four major awards in the arts. This superstar is indeed a national treasure, as evidenced by her being awarded the Presidential Medal of Freedom by President George W. Bush in 2004.

Rita Moreno

GEORGE CHAKIRIS *(Bernardo)*

George Chakiris

ALTHOUGH GEORGE WAS A JET in the London production, he played *Bernardo,* a Shark, in the 1961 movie. As a Jet, I was not allowed to talk to him. *For heaven's sakes, he was my surrogate big brother!* Jerry had firmly laid down the rules while we were filming. No fraternizing between Jets and Sharks. Should we get caught, our threatened penalty would be buying breakfast for the crew. I mean the entire crew. Catered! That would have been the better part of $1,200 or more. *Yikes!*

While in Hollywood, George called one Sunday and invited me over to share a pot of spaghetti with Rita Moreno and her boyfriend. After dinner, we decided to go to the movies. *The Seventh Seal* was playing at the cinema on Hollywood Boulevard. I happened to mention that, should we have to stand in line at the theatre, "You all would have to shield me if anyone from the Studio happens by."

Getting caught fraternizing with the Sharks could be expensive. With their assurance that they would shield me, we had a lovely evening... except for the movie. The *Seventh Seal* is depressing as hell. And I didn't get it! We went back to George's and talked the night away. Rita's boyfriend didn't chat much. Impressive guy though. His name: Marlon Brando. Yeah, that Marlon Brando—the one who won the Academy Award for best actor — twice!

George and Rita both won Academy Awards for their outstanding performances in *West Side Story.*

ROBERT WISE, CO-DIRECTOR

R OBERT WISE WAS QUIET AND FOCUSED, easy to talk to, and unassuming. I had no idea about the movie history behind this man when I was signed on to do the film. He was co-director with Jerry, which I thought was smart given the fact that Jerry had never directed a Hollywood movie.

In 1941, Wise was nominated for an Academy Award for editing the classic *Citizen Kane*. He directed *The Body Snatcher* in '45, *The Day the Earth Stood Still* in '51, *Run Silent, Run Deep* in '58, and *I Want to Live* in '58. He would win an Academy Award for directing two musicals, *West Side Story* and *The Sound of Music*. There was no limit to his ability to jump from one genre to another.

Left to right: ***David Bean, David Winters, Eliot Feld, Tony Mordente, Robert Wise, Tucker Smith, Bert Michaels, Bobby Banas, Harvey Evans, Tom Abbott, Scooter Teague***

Over the months we were together, I found Robert Wise very easy to work with. Cool, calm, and collected. On the other hand, Jerry was emotional and pensive at times; you had to be at the top of your game with him.

As we were nearing the end of filming, we were told that Jerry was not coming back. If there was a reason that Jerry was fired (other than his excessive perfectionism which led him to budget overruns), none of the dancers were involved in the decision to let him go. This is not to say that we were all super-shocked by this turn of events.

With the exception of the *Dance at the Gym,* all the dance numbers were in the can. Tony Mordente and Tommy Abbott were given the job of finishing the *Dance at the Gym* from a dancer's perspective. Robert Wise was still directing and in command.

Soon after the "Dance Hall" segment, we were finished. Mr. Wise called me in to his office and asked what my future plans were.

"I have an offer from London," I replied, "to take *West Side Story* on a British tour." Mr. Wise paused for a moment and then said, "If you want to stay here, David, I have two projects I'm working on. One, a Western and the other a war film with Steve McQueen called *The Sand Pebbles.* There is a part for you in both of these if you want it." Man, I must have been sure of myself. My immediate response was, "Mr. Wise, have you ever seen me on a horse? I look absolutely ridiculous on a horse, and touring England in *West Side Story* is what I think I want to do!"

What? Touring England? Am I crazy? Turn down a Steve McQueen film? Good grief, I could have been a cowboy star...What was I thinking?

Thinking? No, I wasn't thinking. I was reacting. It was hormonal. Jean was in England and there was no doubt my body was headed on a straight hormonal path to London and the British touring production of *West Side Story* and, of course, Miss Jean Deeks.

Jerry

HIS NAME is Jerome Robbins. Some called him one of the greatest choreographers of all time. Everyone called him Jerry. The man's legacy of dance and musical theatre will surely bless the world for generations. The respect he commanded was legend, yet no one called him Mr. Robbins. It was always *Jerry*.

Writing about one's past is cathartic. You discover how your past has developed your future — and how you became the person you are today, and who it was that helped to mold your character.

Jerry is an enormous part of my metamorphosis. Sadly, I don't recall ever saying *thank you*. Not verbally anyway. But I like to think that my thanks was there in every move he asked for... from the top, on stage, or in rehearsal. Jerry changed my life and, in a fashion, was a part of my lifelong 180 Rule. Working for Jerry over a period of eight years, I always sought to give him 180%.

I wish he were here. I would give him a hug and tell him how grateful I am — and then listen for that giggle-laugh that indicated we were right with the world and on the right path.

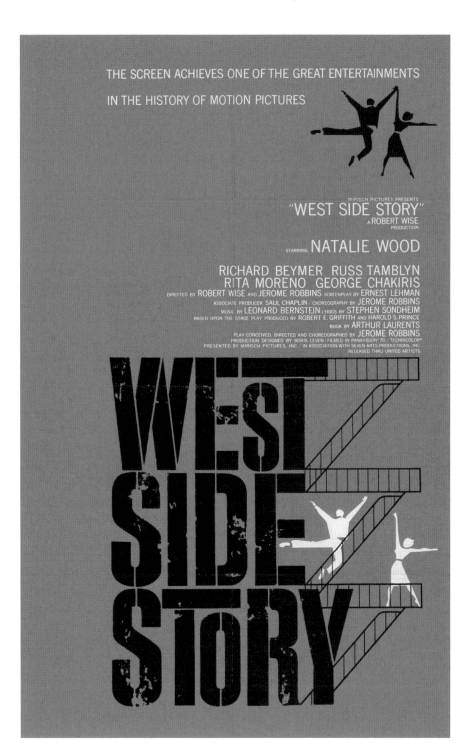

50th Anniversary Musical Encore *for* West Side Story

FIFTY YEARS AFTER the release of the movie, the New York Philharmonic Orchestra played the entire score of *West Side Story* at the Alice Tully Hall—in sync with the movie being shown on a screen above the orchestra. David Newman conducted and several of the cast members were in the audience.

The evening was transcendent. During an intermission, Russ Tamblyn, George Chakiris, Eddie Verso, Bert Michaels, Harvey Evans and I were introduced. The audience erupted in cheers. We were a surprise bonus, as they certainly didn't expect our appearance a half-century later!

The musical celebration was repeated around the world, commemorating 50 years of *West Side.* But they apparently forgot to invite the Jets and Sharks for those additional worldwide performances in 2011. Pity, it would have been great fun.

Nonetheless, four of us were invited to the Tanglewood Music Center for a repeat 50th Anniversary celebration, conducted once again by David Newman. We gave a TV interview and sat on a panel for a sponsors' luncheon at Seranak, the former summer home of BSO conductor Serge Koussevitzky.

David Bean, Eddie Verso,
Harvey Evans, Bert Michaels

Opening in Bristol with my mate Jean

> *In early February 1961, I caught the first plane to London. Jean did greet me at Heathrow Airport and that's when my life really began. A new mate, a reason to get up every morning and truly be in love. I was a goner! Hook, line and sinker.*

~7~

West Side Story
(British Tour)

DOLLY

REHEARSALS BEGAN in February 1961 at Her Majesty's Theatre. The West End production of *West Side Story* was still playing, giving us the use of the sets. On Saturday, we worked at the Drury Lane Theatre. Both of these theatres were in London, within easy commuting by "tube" from Greenford, where we were staying with Jean's parents. Jean's brother Barry gave up his bedroom, poor sod, as I stayed with the Deeks family during the pre-tour rehearsals.

Our first tour date was at the Streatham Hill Theatre, not too far from London — and we would drive Dad's car to the performances.

All well and good, but what about the rest of the tour? We needed a car. Dad's Renault had to stay with him in Greenford.

On a very chilly evening after rehearsals, we arrived home in Greenford. Mum, Dad and Barry were waiting for us on the front stoop. " 'Ello love!" As the normal greetings took place, Mum added, " 'Ere Mates, come 'ave a look at this!"

We all followed her. Still in her house slippers, she led us to Jean's Uncle Len's garage, across the street. Most of Jean's aunts and uncles lived within a block or so. Uncle Len and Auntie Edie had a garage, very posh! The street was damp and icy and we needed a torch (flash light) to navigate the fifty yards to Uncle Len's. It took a couple of minutes to pry the heavy wooden gates open that hid this tiny garage behind the massive gates. "Open the door, Love." As Mum pointed her light on the garage doors, Barry and Dad each opened the doors like a grand stage production

"Ta–da" they sang out — and there she was, the saddest looking tiny black car, with one of its headlights leaning to one side on top of the fender. While the grill seemed to force a smile in the somewhat dim light of Mum's torch.

"Oh my!" The exclamations were filling the air. *"Does it run?"*

Dolly, our 1932 Austin 7

"Yes, like a clock" Dad said. You won't find a better one for twelve pounds, mate!"

"Twelve pounds?" (that was roughly $2.80 to the pound or $34.00)! Though the car clearly needed a bit of work, Dad assured us that we could get it finished and ready for our tour by the end of the Streatham Hill engagement. And so it was. We had transport, as sad as she looked, our enthusiasm was not deterred. "'Er Mate, she needs a name." "'ow about Dolly?" Jean's mother was Dorothy Ivy Deeks. Many called her Doll, and now we had "Dolly," a 1932 Austin 7. *Perfect!*

While we continued rehearsals at Her Majesty's Theatre and the Drury Lane Theater, Jean's dad, Ernie, put in motion the incredible family restoration of Dolly! Uncle Len was a machinist and replaced the roof and mended the push-out front window. Uncle Fred worked at Aladdin Heater Factory; he painted the entire car white. Uncle Boy cleaned and polished the spokes on all four wheels. Ernie made metal parts for the windows, which now worked up and down like new. I helped Dad rewire the entire car. We did nothing with the motor. It really did run like a top. We were now ready to begin our eleven-month British tour.

BRISTOL

OFF TO BRISTOL. As we set our luggage in the rear seat of the car, the entire family was gathered on the sidewalk — waving and shouting best wishes as we pulled away in our bright white "Dolly" for a journey that would last the entire year of 1961. We would put 3,000 miles on Dolly — with a top speed of 41 miles an hour, and giving us 51 miles to the gallon. (Mind you, the top speed of 41 mph was achieved only when going down hill, with a lovely tailwind!)

Heading southwest, our little Austin 7 — with its seven horsepower engine and cable brakes — performed handsomely. Bristol is a charming town with shops tucked into the center of town which must have been built three hundred years ago. Across from our theatre stage door was the original home of Bristol Sherry and Liquors. Very handy. We always

AFTER THE RUMBLE
David Holliday (Tony) and Jean Deeks (Anybodys)

kept a pint of Bristol Cream Sherry in the dressing room. Having a nip before curtain was essential for relaxing the vocal chords. *"What?"* you say. Ah yes, we were dancers...dancers who sang a little.

Jeanie played *Anybodys* in our touring production. She was a pixie and just delightful with her American, mostly Southern, accent. She would sooner have been a Shark girl and danced *America* (which she did back at Her Majesty's Theatre while in the London production). Jean's original position when hired was to be the versatile *Swing Girl*. It's a difficult job, since the Swing must know everyone's part — Jet *and* Shark. If Jean went on for a Shark girl, she dyed her hair black. Otherwise she was a flaming redhead. The part of *Anybodys* required much less dancing.

COVENTRY

OUR DRIVE TO COVENTRY was a challenge with Dolly. The car battery would not charge and getting there was a trip from hell. Every time little Dolly's engine stopped, we had to push her and pop the clutch to get her going again. We charged the battery, but it wouldn't hold the charge. Finally, we arrived in Coventry. Five of us in the cast booked digs at a working farm.

The farmhouse was early 1700s, enclosed by a beautiful eight-foot brick wall, protecting an English garden to die for. This was fun stuff, living on the farm, making friends with the animals. "Oxo" was an eighteen-month old heifer that befriended Jean. Was it Jean's good looks that attracted Oxo? Or was it the bucket of oats she dutifully promised on her morning visit?!

While in Coventry, we decided to have Dolly checked over. We found a handy Lucas Light repair shop. Driving her in was like wheeling a pram with a new baby into a supermarket. They fawned over Dolly like old hens.

First, her dynamo was not working properly. In "American talk," that's the generator. From Birmingham, they found a dynamo from 1932, still in its original box. They rewired the entire electrical system making Dolly good as new. We expected to pay handsomely but were gifted the entire job citing the joy Dolly brought into their shop. In return, we bought everyone in the shop a season ticket to the Coventry Theatre. Bolstered by the TLC Dolly received from our Lucas Light chaps, she drove us effortlessly.

Touring in England had its challenges with each theatre. Most of the stages are raked; they slope upwards, away from the audience. To dance on a raked stage takes extra practice. One night, at the end of the *Prologue,* all the Jets were supposed to "cluster center," near the footlights, to sing the *Jet Song.* But this night, only two of us were in position to cover the dialogue and sing, which we did. *What happened to the guys?* We were perplexed.

It turns out that the stage rake was slightly higher back to front. With all our intense dancing in *West Side Story,* the bolts, holding the set together, popped out — and the set came racing down to the footlights. The kids on stage stopped the set from plowing into the orchestra pit, pulled it upstage and held it while the two of us sang the *Jet Song.*

OXFORD

W E RENTED A CABIN CRUISER on the River Isis which runs through the town of Oxford. Our home on the Isis/Thames was called the *Gray Wake*. Living on the River in 1961 was simple. There seemed to be no restrictions. We could moor wherever we wanted each night.

The boat had a galley and room to sleep four. While performing in Oxford, David Holliday and Carol Gray shared the four weeks living on the River. Carol played *Anita* in the show and David was *Tony*. Had Jerry Robbins been there at the time, *Tony* (a Jet) and *Anita* (a Shark) would not have been allowed to share the same space. Since Jerry wasn't there, we all enjoyed each other's mixed company, boating up and down and through the locks of the River. The early morning swans would wake us—not appreciating the late nights we kept.

Hosting a party on the Gray Wake, *Oxford, 1961*

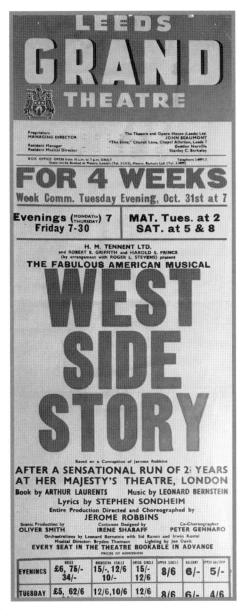

LEEDS TO BLACKPOOL

OUR NEXT MOVE was to Leeds in the northeast. We booked our digs in a home of a recently widowed man who did all the cooking. His specialty was roast beef and Yorkshire pudding. Turns out his *only* cooking talent was roast beef and Yorkshire pudding. After a week, we started eating out.

We traveled from Leeds to Manchester and on to Blackpool, known for the *Blackpool Illuminations,* their magnificent annual lights festival. A seaside town with a wonderful Winter Garden Theatre, it also featured a fun zone for vacationers, with a roller coaster and other rides. We ended up staying in an apartment with no heat. Arriving in our digs after the show, we were greeted by a freezing apartment. So, the first thing we did was turn on the oven to warm up the place. It was simple and effective, with one drawback. The apartment walls would sweat. The very first night, we left the bed against the wall. *A serious mistake!* By morning, the bed clothes were soaking wet. Pushing the bed into the middle of the room was the only solution.

GLASGOW

GLASGOW, SCOTLAND WAS NEXT. Two kids in the show, Bernie and Earl, found two caravans not far from the theatre and Jean and I were kindly offered one. In the United States, these caravans would be called trailers. They were tiny units — not a space you'd want to live in for six weeks. The location of our two caravans was on a private horse track. Inside the painted white fence was a dirt track, and the horses were very happy on the inside. *Rightly so.* Jean and Bernie were their frequent benefactors, supplying bushels of carrots and apples.

Our source of heat in the caravan was propane and, just as in Blackpool, it tended to make the walls sweat; but by this time we didn't seem to mind. Jean frightened me to death one morning when jumping out of bed to make the morning cuppa. The burner didn't light and the resulting explosion blew her eyebrows off along with the front of her hair. The bang was bigger than the burn and she survived to make a proper cuppa. Thank you, Typhoo tea and Max Factor.

Glasgow isn't too far from a tiny town called Gretna Green, the Las Vegas of Scotland for impromptu marriages. Although there was no gambling in Gretna Green, you certainly could get a "quickie marriage" there. It was indeed a popular place for shotgun weddings. Jean's parents, Dolly and Ern, had been writing us all through the tour, keeping in touch. One particular letter was rather touching as they wrote: "Since you two are so near Gretna Green, why don't you sneak down and secretly get married. We promise, we won't tell anyone!" How sweet! Of course, our reply was prompt. "It's *you* we're not supposed to tell!" We did laugh.

We celebrated Christmas and the final days of 1961 in Glasgow. The four of us "caravaners" — Jean, myself, Bernie and Earl — booked New Year's Eve at a ski resort in Kilan, 90 miles northeast of Glasgow. Early Sunday morning, we set out in Bernie's car to see the New Year in at this quaint ski resort. Scotland is not the first place that comes to mind when planning a ski holiday, but there it was, tucked into a beautiful setting with four feet of snow. A dozen or more skis standing in the snow just outside the Inn. Of course, we didn't ski. We checked in and then spent an hour having snowball fights while frolicking in the snow until dinnertime. *Cheers for a memorable 1961 and a promising 1962.*

EDINBURGH

EDINBURGH WAS OUR LAST STOP ON THE TOUR. Again we rented digs—this time from a chap named Tony Ferry. Tony made Scott's Porage Oats every morning with a dollop of Tate & Lyle Golden syrup. His kitchen had a stove fueled by wood, cozy and warm as toast. A fond memory that floods back at the very thought of Scott's Porage Oats and Tony Ferry.

BACK TO LONDON

THE TOUR WAS MAGICAL—a year of wonderful memories and our fantastic courtship. We were excited to travel back to London and make plans for our wedding. To this day, Jean is so happy she had a chance to see her own country and enjoy the many adventures we had before the wedding. . . . To paraphrase a song:

> *"Jeanie Deeks is a pretty nice girl, some day I'm going to make her mine. Jeanie Deeks is a pretty nice girl, but she changes from day to day. I want to tell her that I love her a lot, and I don't need to get a belly full of wine. Jeanie Deeks is a pretty nice girl, some day I'm gonna make her mine, oh yeah — some day I'm gonna make her mine."* **Thank you, Beatles.** *That "some day" did arrive: March 24, 1962.*

DAVID & JEAN
Holy Trinity, Knightsbridge
London, March 24, 1962

~ 8 ~

Our Wedding

CYRIL WAS MY BEST MAN. A couple of days before the wedding, he flew into London. I was booted out of the Deeks' family house and my best man and I went to a hotel just down the road from the church in Knightsbridge.

"Where is this Holy Trinity?" Cyril asked.

"It's just down the block from Harrods in Knightsbridge," I replied. Knowing that Cyril had attended Mass at the Oratory there for years, I asked him, "Do you know where the Brompton Oratory is?" (I also knew that Cyril's brother Edgar had painted one of the Brompton Oratory chapels using the three-dimensional art technique, *tromp l'oeil*.)

"Well," I continued, "if you follow the beautiful tree-lined lane running alongside the Oratory, you'll find Holy Trinity down that lane behind your Catholic Church!"

"Oh," Cyril said, in his chirpy, winning English accent. "The church behind the better one!"

On the other side of town, Jean and her entourage were busy primping and prepping with excited anticipation befitting a Cockney family preparing for an evening with the Queen. Far from an average day at the Deeks' household, the hour was at hand for the Princess to be whisked away on her forty-minute ride to Knightsbridge.

Dad quickly befriended the limo driver and the chat for most of the drive to Knightsbridge was about the race track and the gee-gees (horses).

127

As arrival time neared, the driver pulled the car to the side of the road explaining; "I've been driving brides to their weddings for ten years, and I've never got one of 'em to the church on time. I don't reckon to spoil me record today, mate."

They sat there for twenty minutes talking horses. The bride was twenty minutes late.

In the meantime, Cyril and I had been standing by the altar, waiting for the bride to waltz down the aisle on the arm of her father. Anticipating the start of the wedding march, Cyril nudged me to turn and look at the back of the church. There we could see two small figures behind the glass doors leading into the nave of the church. The bride and her father were standing tall at five-feet each. Several times, Jean disappeared from view on the other side of the opaque glass door — and then magically reappeared to her dad's height, then slowly down and out of sight again. *My God, she is warming up — grand pliés behind glass doors!*

Jean's walk down the aisle was beautiful. Her father held her hand out as if presenting her to the world each step of the way down the double-wide aisle. Guests were seated in the choir stall near the altar, and as we joined hands facing the altar we were given a hymnal. Before a word was spoken we sang.

This "first act" in song was brilliant and magical; and, as a result, all tension was gone, and we were able to relax and take in the entire ceremony. It didn't hurt that our guest list included several cast members from *West Side Story,* as well as West End show folks who were very much at home belting out a hymn — to everyone's delight.

As we were pronounced Mr. & Mrs. Bean, the sun appeared as though on cue, filling the church with light from the magnificent stained glass windows above the altar.

After stepping into the rectory to sign the register, the guests were then asked to file down each side of the extra-wide aisle in the middle of the church and the new Mr. and Mrs. waltzed through the line in Hollywood film fashion.

The reception at the Vanderbilt Hotel was simple and charming—tea sandwiches of cucumber and salmon, lots of champagne, and lots of happy people, especially my mother.

It all ended far too soon for Jean and me — because Cyril decided it was time for us to leave. We were literally ushered out of our own reception! Outside the hotel was "Dolly," waiting to take us to Brighton. The "just married" sign was still on the boot of the car which made for an eventful drive to Brighton. We arrived at three in the afternoon. Much too early.

What to do? Hard to believe, but we found ourselves in the local cinema watching *El Cid.* After the movie, we stopped at a local restaurant for tea where there was a wedding reception in progress. It was still only six-ish, so we joined in, never mentioning we had only just tied the knot ourselves that morning.

"Dolly" in the wings

We arrived at the Royal Crescent Hotel, checking into the honeymoon suite for a week, a gift to us from Cyril. The suite was filled with white flowers and champagne. Thanks to Cyril, we thoroughly enjoyed it — *carte blanche* for the entire week — including the hotel's four-star restaurant.

Our suite had French doors opening out to a balcony overlooking the pebbled beaches of Brighton and the Channel (*English Channel, of course*). Beautiful tea sandwiches and champagne and we were in for the night.

Left to right: *Jean's Dad: Ernie Deeks; David's Mom: Merle Bean; the Groom; the Bride; Jean's Mum: Dolly Deeks; the Best Man: Cyril Ritchard.*

~ 9 ~

Return to New York

WHILE ON OUR HONEYMOON, a surprise call came from Cyril, offering us a wonderful performance opportunity. But it gave us little time to pack up and be in New York by early April.

Cyril would be portraying *Phileas Fogg* in Mike Todd Jr's. musical production of *Around the World in 80 Days.* Jean and I would be the principal dancers and each have a small bit part, joining Cyril as *Phileas,* Pierre Olaf as *Passepartout,* Jan McArt as *Aouda* and Dom DeLuise as *Detective Fix.* A terrific cast. Ted Cappy would choreograph the show. How super it was to have the opportunity to receive a paycheck as we started our life's journey together. We gathered our belongings from over the past year and shipped them to New York. We landed in the City ready to work.

At the time, Cyril had a "gentleman's gentleman," Eddie Parr. He was a friendly, slight fellow, kept busy dressing Cyril in the theatre, taking care of odds and ends, driving him and, seeing to his overall needs.

It was Eddie who picked us up at Kennedy Airport and drove us to 135 Central Park West where we would live in Cyril's guest room as newlyweds for the next few months. Jean could hardly speak for the pomp of it all. Someone to greet us at the airport, drive us first class in a beautiful '58 Cadillac convertible, for arrival at a very posh apartment on Central Park West, overlooking the City's iconic Central Park.

Wow! For a girl from Greenford, Middlesex, it was overwhelming to say the least. Jean's introduction to New York City must have been exciting and terrifying all at the same time. After settling in the apartment I couldn't wait to show her the City...New York in all its glory.

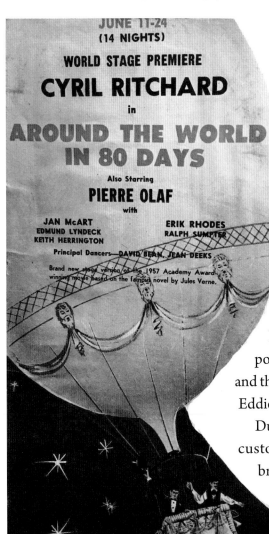

JUNE 11-24
(14 NIGHTS)

WORLD STAGE PREMIERE

CYRIL RITCHARD

in

AROUND THE WORLD IN 80 DAYS

Also Starring

PIERRE OLAF

with

JAN McART   ERIK RHODES
EDMUND LYNDECK   RALPH SUMPTER
KEITH HERRINGTON

Principal Dancers—DAVID BEAN, JEAN DEEKS

Brand new stage version of the 1957 Academy Award-winning movie based on the famous novel by Jules Verne.

AROUND THE WORLD IN 80 DAYS

OUR FIRST STOP with *80 Days* was St. Louis. We drove the Wolseley out and settled in with rehearsals at the Muny Theatre, America's oldest and largest outdoor musical theatre. It was hot and we spent equal time rehearsing and in the hotel pool. Jean still couldn't swim, and that summer she learned with Eddie Parr's help.

During these rehearsals. it was customary to horse around on breaks. Pierre Olaf, as Passe-partout, carried a carpetbag as part of his character. Clowning around, Jean (weighing all of 105 pounds) got into the bag — and Pierre carried her about. As part of the scene, he stopped at customs while going on the world trip — and Jean would pop out of the carpetbag. They wrote this skit into the performance and Dom DeLuise, Pierre and Jean had a running shtick throughout the tour for laughs.

Mr. Herbert O. ("H.O.") Peet, of the retail giant, Palmolive Peet, was a large supporter of the Muny opera. I somehow received an invitation to play golf with his wife Margot at their very posh country club. *Ah! Here we go boys, a pro course with fairways equal to the greens. I'll have to be a gentleman—and go easy on Margot.*

What was I thinking? She crushed me every time we played. She had class — and a fabulous golf game. Did I mention that I was 22, and she a very spry 60-something?

Jean, Cyril and I were invited to lunch at their incredible Tudor home. H.O. was in the pool sitting on a ledge with a mint julep in his hand when we arrived. Within minutes, we were all in the pool. I swam up to the ledge and sat next to H.O. "How's biz?" I offered up.

"We're doing fine, young man. But according to my wife, you might do well if you stick to dancing and not entertain the idea of becoming a golf pro." We laughed . . . and he had another mint julep. I ate humble pie!

Brooklyn Heights

Jean and I were still living with Cyril at Central Park West; and for some reason we decided to look for our own apartment. Our search for new digs brought us to Brooklyn Heights. We found a tiny apartment that had great potential. At $125 a month, we took a gulp and signed a lease. In those days, $125 was just about what you brought home doing a Broadway show. Understandably, Jean was nervous about the challenge. Her entire life kept getting flipped overnight.

Our new apartment allowed us to plunge into our life together as an independent couple. We started with the renovation of our apartment. First, we removed all the plaster from the living room wall, which exposed the underlayment of brick. Replacing a window in our bedroom with a door gave us access to the roof, which we made into a terrace overlooking our neighbor's garden. The terrace was larger than our apartment.

Arriving in America after our wedding, we had foolishly decided not to take any Broadway show offers unless we were both in the show.

Returning to NYC in the fall after *Around the World in 80 Days,* auditions came and went. We both were offered work individually, but always turned it down, keeping with our decision to only work together. *Oops!* By November we were out of work. Being poor brings out the best in you. We never ate out and Jean was a genius in the kitchen. Every night we ate gourmet meals. Think about it! Four eggs, a bit of cheese, "voila" a soufflé! Add a 75 cent loaf of French bread, a bottle of 99 cent Pouilly Fuisse and you are in culinary heaven.

Jean would stop at the butcher's and get beef hearts and lamb shanks for under a dollar each. *Brilliant!* Jean's good looks were helpful. The butcher would kindly save her some savory bits of meat. She was coming home with outrageous deals . . . until the butcher followed her home one day. We put an end to that catch of the day!

ABRAHAM & STRAUSS DEPARTMENT STORE

I DON'T REMEMBER HOW IT CAME ABOUT, but our next job was at Abraham & Strauss in Brooklyn. We couldn't do Christmas without a job. So there we were, employees of A&S. Jean worked at the jewelry counter and I managed the Santa Claus department. We had five Santas to handle the crowd. My job was to usher the children into the Santa cubicle where a photo was taken and then usher them out. My instructions: "Do not touch the children. Keep your hands behind your back and talk, talk, talk. Never touch." There are mothers who make a profession out of preying on other people to make a living. *Terrifying!*

One of our Santas was an old gentleman's gentleman who worked for Van Johnson. He was a perfect Santa. One morning, when he called in sick, I had to go on in his place. It's theatre and I was his understudy. This in itself was ludicrous. To begin with, I weighed 160 pounds, had obnoxious red hair, and couldn't resonate *ho, ho, ho* without putting my thumb to my teeth. The next day I was given a rejected photo of three small children clinging onto me screaming, with my red hair clearly visible under my wig.

Jean, on the floor below, was solving her own shortcomings. Having failed the "eleven plus" exam (at the end of British primary school), her counting ability on registers was on the slow side. She was more successful counting on her fingers behind her back.

One morning, we were late for work. Jean explained there was a fire in the Tube. Her supervisor looked puzzled and asked, "A fire in the *what?*"

"The Tube," Jean said. Her supervisor marched straight to the first firebox and pulled the alarm. "What floor?" she shouted as the entire store was clanging with the sound of the fire alarm.

"No, no, no, the *subway!* Not the tubes in the store!" If you have never seen them, back in the day, money was sent by vacuum tubes from each register station to an office somewhere in the building. The Fire Department cleared the building that morning, giving everyone in the building a three-hour break.

By the end of January, we were out of work again and very happy to be auditioning! We wisely dropped our stipulation about working together in shows. Jean started rehearsal for the revival of *The Boys from Syracuse.*

PRISONER OF ZENDA

IT WASN'T LONG before we hit the boards again; both of us auditioned and were hired by choreographer Onna White to do *The Prisoner of Zenda,* with Chita Rivera and Alfred Drake. Rehearsals started in Los Angeles, the play opened in San Francisco, then back to Los Angeles, and then on to Broadway. Jean was cast as one of the "Rasendyll Girls."

Arriving in Los Angeles, we were greeted with the news: Onna White had been fired and Jack Cole was now the choreographer. We were all under contract so Jack Cole had, like it or not, inherited a cast of Onna White dancers. Jean is a Jack Cole dancer. I'm not. Like Bob Fosse, Jack's movements are tiny and, well, itty-bitty at times. I don't do itty-bitty. Jerome Robbins hired me, Donald Saddler hired me, but Jack Cole would never hire me. Yet here I was a Jack Cole dancer…that hurt a lot. Our first ten days were learning how to be a Jack Cole dancer.

Without a doubt, Jack Cole had a wonderful body of work. His dance credits include work you may be familiar with, including *Some Like It Hot* and *Gentlemen Prefer Blondes,* both with my old friend Marilyn Monroe. *Kismet,* with Alfred Drake, *The Merry Widow, Gilda, Man of La Mancha,* and, one of our favorite movies, *Les Girls.*

Our rehearsals took place in the NBC Studio in Hollywood. We were not the only company working there. One afternoon, Sammy Davis Jr. wandered into our rehearsal. Back in Manchester, England in 1958, he had spent time in the wings watching our production of *West Side Story.* He loved the show and loved being there. I reminded him of that and within minutes we were tap dancing. This man had incredible rhythm. I'm a good hoofer, but keeping up with Sammy Davis?! *No way!* Our entire throw-down didn't last more than fifteen minutes, but those minutes are logged into my memory forever.

San Francisco was super. Jean and I rented an apartment with a Murphy bed and we bought a tiny two-pound baby toy dachshund, "Count Rudolfus of Zenda Bean." Tom John, the scene designer, wrote us an illustrated letter of "Count Rudy" with a title, "Isn't it nice to have royalty in the family!"

Working again with Chita Rivera was a joy. Her heart is as big as all outdoors . . . her talent bigger. Marc Wilder made a perfect dance partner for her. Jack Cole gave them beautiful work. It was something to watch. During a

Jean and Count Rudolfus

performance one evening in San Francisco, I was in the middle of a dance number with Marc and Chita when we had a simple knee slide choreographed in the number. I hit the floor in my slide and *pow!* My left knee exploded. The tendons had yanked out of the "soft spot" in my lower femur. My knee swelled up like a balloon and the pain nearly knocked me out. I was out of commission and promptly transported to Los Angeles for surgery.

The medical procedure was to pack the soft spot in the leg bone (femur) with bone from my hip. I now have a cute, rather large, dimple in my hip; and my left leg became stronger than my right. During my hospital stay, I had relatively little pain and was healing fast. Jeanie would visit daily and then go off to the Philharmonic Theater in Los Angeles to do the show.

One daily visit, Jean brought my mother. She also brought me a surprise goodie to eat for later. I opened the package to find what should have been a candy apple. All of the red sugar coating had softened and slid to one side forming a goiter-looking appendage on the apple. Now I was looking at an apple with a stick in it! "I made you a candy apple!" Jean professed.

"You did?"

We started to laugh. It soon became contagious. Getting the giggles is one thing, belly laughs are painful. Both my wife and my mother were disappearing below the end of the bed. I do believe Jean wet the floor. The chap in the bed next to me was screaming, "Stop, stop!" The poor guy had recently married and had to be circumcised. You can't make these things up. The fact I had little to no pain myself was shortlived. I had torn the stitches in my hip and had to be medicated. Jean was politely asked not to bring me any additional surprises.

Within two weeks, I was walking pretty well. I went back into the show — a small part, no dancing.

Alfred Drake was the man. His energy was always up and he worked tirelessly! One evening, the actor and singer had been given new lyrics — very fast and complicated, written by Martin Charnin. In the middle of the song, Alfred sang the wrong lyric and literally stopped the orchestra. Breaking character, he addressed the audience, "Ladies and Gentlemen, this lyric was just given to me this afternoon. With your permission I'm going to sing it until I get it right!"

The audience stood in applause. How wonderful for them to be in on the mishap.

Anne Rogers was *Princess Flavia*. She had a beautiful voice and we loved her. It is strange how the turn of events shape our lives. Anne was starring in *The Boy Friend* in London when *My Fair Lady* was written. They were scouting for the lead, *Eliza Doolittle,* and the songwriting team of Alan J. Lerner & Frederick Loewe wanted Anne for the part.

Her employers would not let her out of her contract. So they auditioned her understudy, Julie Andrews.

For reasons I can only imagine (but really don't have a clue), *Prisoner of Zenda* closed in Los Angeles. We never came to Broadway!

On our flight back home to New York, Jean and I learned the very sad news that JFK had been shot. *November 22, 1963.*

To Broadway With Love

JEAN AND I AUDITIONED for Morton DaCosta and Donald Saddler who had been hired for the 1964 World's Fair musical production of *To Broadway with Love.* Billed as "the musical of the century," the show featured 100 years of American musical theatre. We had two complete casts of 80 members. The "East Company, " which included Jean and me, would perform three shows a day and have the next day off! "The West Company" would perform three shows on our day off. One day on, one day off. Jean was a featured player in the cast and did three numbers. One number with Eddie Roll (Eddie was in the original Broadway show, as well as the London production of *West Side Story*).

Eddie Roll and Jean Deeks in To Broadway with Love

With three numbers to perform in the show, Jean had three costume changes. I did eight dance numbers with eight costume changes. Jean was paid $1,000 a week and I received $300. It wasn't fair! We complained to each other all the way to the bank.

Working with choreographer Donald Saddler was a highlight worth writing about. We recreated a dance number from the movie, *Lullaby of Broadway*. A movie screen was dropped above us on stage and the original film was shown. We replicated it onstage below the screen. The staircase was reproduced and all the dancers tapped their way through the number in sync with the movie. In the movie, the tap-dancing Condos Brothers (Steve, Nick and Frank) did an unbelievable break in the middle of the number; three of us met their challenge live on stage. We had to recreate each step from the screen, which meant watching the film close-up in rehearsal and match it! The number was spectacular. It was the best thing in the show for me.

Living in Brooklyn Heights meant we rode the subway to Flushing (where the old Shea Stadium stood) and then walked two miles to the Texas Pavilion, all the way across the fairgrounds. If we walked, we saved a dollar on bus fare.

Between shows (remember, we did three shows a day), we cooked in the dressing rooms. All the kids did. It was way too expensive to eat at the Fair. After the show, we walked back across the fairgrounds to the subway. Our grand intention to save money was honorable until the walk home. You see, we had to pass the Schaefer Pavilion; therein lies the folly. *To Broadway with Love* — to home with Schaefer beer.

The show didn't do well at the box office. We were located on the other side of the Long Island Expressway and the foot traffic was minimal. They even brought in Eydie Gormé to sing between shows to attract attention. But it didn't work. The show only ran for the 1964 summer. It lost $11,000,000 in the process. That was huge in 1964.

~ 10 ~

Fifty Miles

HOUSE-HUNTING

WHEN WORKING ON BROADWAY, most contracts require one to live within 50 miles of the city. Now that we were flush from our last job, *To Broadway with Love,* we could go through the *New York Times* real estate ads and only look for something within 50 miles.

Our first phone call in the fall of '64 was for viewing a house near Peekskill, NY. We called and the owner made arrangements to pick us up at the Peekskill train station. He met us and drove ten miles east of Peekskill to a hamlet called Shrub Oak. The house was among 80+ summer homes built by garment workers out of New York City. All of these summer homes had now been winterized.

The home we were about to see was a Frank Lloyd Wright design. Plans for the home were bought from the '39 World's Fair. Nice touch, as it was the '64 World's Fair that made all this house-hunting possible.

The house was on two acres on a hill overlooking Putnam Valley. The property was on several levels, all landscaped beautifully and very private. The community had a beautiful six-acre lake with a club house. Everything seemed magical.

We boarded the Metro train back to New York City, not fully realizing that by giving the owner a $200 check as a binder, we just committed ourselves to a 20-year debt in the form of a mortgage. He had agreed to give us a $5,000 purchase money mortgage to go with our down payment. Our lawyer would handle the details. We couldn't wait to move out of Brooklyn as we had already housed three dogs and an aquarium of neon tetra. The dogs would have a field day on two acres. And we could end our ritual of warning the cockroaches when we arrived home in our Brooklyn Heights apartment; we would clap our hands while singing out, "Party's over, we're home now."

Our attorney had an office on 42nd Street between 6th and 7th Avenues. It was an odd location I thought. We met in his office and you could have blown me over with a feather . . . our attorney was totally blind. He did everything by feel and memory. His secretary made notes and saw to the legal transcripts.

We walked from his office over to Fifth Avenue, heading north to the seller's attorney. As we walked, our lawyer described every building on the block, when it was built and of what! We were impressed.

At the closing, a list of items totaling what we had to pay (fuel oil, taxes, etc.) was given to us. The owner had already paid for them. Normal stuff.

"Wait," our attorney said holding up his hand. "Would you read that column again?" Their attorney did, and you won't believe this: there was an error in the math — which our attorney had calculated in his head — to the tune of $1,200 in our favor!

SHRUB OAK

WE CLOSED ON OUR NEW HOME in Shrub Oak in the summer of 1964. We rented a twenty-foot U-Haul, packed our belongings from Brooklyn Heights, and headed north to a very big change of life.

During this time period, Cyril, knowing we were looking for a house, hoped we'd explore the area, near his country home,

"Lone Rock," in Ridgefield, Connecticut. We simply couldn't afford the Ridgefield area. Cyril wasn't all that thrilled with our move to Shrub Oak, or even the choice of our new home. He did come to see the house soon after we moved; but it was never the topic of conversation on our weekend visits to Ridgefield (which were many, as I was Lone Rock's handyman). And he continued to introduce us as the "newlyweds."

As this new chapter continued, Cyril wasn't a part of our life in Shrub Oak. In one sense, nothing really changed except that our new digs were rarely mentioned! Life went on.

BALLET SCHOOL & CLASSES

Summer Camp: Jeanie's Ballet Troupe

JEAN STARTED UP HER BALLET SCHOOL in the studio of our home. It was a joy to watch Jean teach. Ninety-nine percent of her students were there for fun, and not to build a career in the Royal Academy as Jean had. She taught for fun. If a child's toe wasn't pointed properly after the umpteenth correction, it was okay as long as she held her head up during a plié so her little imaginary crown didn't fall off!

We had started summer camp at one of the local public schools. About 40 boys and girls (ages 8-12) signed up for the camp. Jean had ballet classes for the girls and I took the boys. The boys, however, were given dance numbers and we never mentioned the word ballet! There was a basketball number (to *Sweet Georgia Brown*) and a football routine—just for boys. They never realized they were doing every ballet step in the book. And they did it well. It was great fun for us, and the children.

For our efforts we had a $1,500 bonus which was used to establish a local theatre group, the Yorktown Players. In addition to putting on our own productions (Jean directed *The Fantastics*), the Players brought in outside productions. Their first paid program was Hal Holbrook's *Mark Twain Tonight!* He got the $1,500 and the Yorktown Players were born.

PRINTING

SHORTLY AFTER moving to Shrub Oak, I talked Jean into buying a printing press. My history in printing began in high school. After the run of *Peter Pan* on Broadway, I had returned to Los Angeles and enrolled at Hamilton High School. My counselor gave me a class in print shop, saying that I needed a "fine art." I had just finished a year on Broadway. *What's with the fine art?*

I was a week or so late registering and when I got to print shop class, Mr. Davis, our instructor, was giving a test. Hanging on the wall was a California job case. This is an elongated drawer with multiple compartments holding small lead moveable type. The test was to identify each compartment that housed a letter of the alphabet, lower case letters on the left side, upper case on the right. Each student would take a baton-like wooden stick and point out all the compartments with the appropriate letter. As soon as the entire class had had their turn, I raised my hand.

"Yes?" from Mr. Davis.

"I can do that."

"You just came in, you don't have to," he informed me.

"Well, I can do it."

"OK, what's your name again?"

I nailed it! I had memorized the entire box in an hour. Truly, I fell in love with printing from the first day. Learning to set type and lock up forms, register the pins on the platen press and to actually ink up and print something was sheer delight. This was old school letterpress printing and the press we ultimately bought was a Kluge automatic platen press. It arrived disassembled, accompanied by two men from New York City who were there to put it together in Jean's laundry room. It was beautiful. I waxed the outer moving parts.

Printing the **Pennysaver** *—*
I loved the smell of ink!

My first job was to produce numbered raffle tickets for a local women's club. They were to be sold for a prize given at a smorgasbord dinner dance. Only one problem: I spelled smorgasbord with a "g" at the end — and they rejected the lot. *Smorgasborg.* I've always pronounced it with a "g" on the end. *Who knew?* I had to reprint the entire job!

As time passed, I added a Chief 15 offset press, built a light table, and installed a Goodkin camera. It was super. Up a short flight of stairs in the foyer was our offset printing shop leading into the laundry room with the Kluge and complete letterpress shop. The top portion of the house was our living quarters. We were now custodians of a Ballet School and a printing business, as well as running into New York City to do TV and Broadway.

DELI DEAL

DAVE AND GUS WERE OUR IMMEDIATE NEIGHBORS. They ran the local Shrub Oak German deli, housed in a building that was for sale. It was during a conversation in the deli that Dave and Gus prompted us to call the owner of the property, Alex Martin. He arrived at our house on a beautiful summer day.

"Hey, we know you," we said, "you're the gardener for the corner property." It was gracious of him to come to our home as he was on his way to "meet with a prospective buyer" and collect a $30,000 down payment check.

"Exactly what are they buying?" I asked.

"They're interested in the entire corner which includes the deli, post office with three apartments above, a building with three businesses along the back, and a separate house on the lot next door."

That was a lot of real estate.

"Why are you selling it?" We were curious.

"I'm getting older," he offered, "and I can't take care of it the way I'd like to anymore."

"Do you need the money?" I asked.

"No, I don't," he said, "I just can't keep up with it."

That's when my business experience kicked in.

"Are you aware," I continued "that your $30,000 check will be worth $15,000 when you get home and remove it from your pocket?" I continued with my business knowledge.

"It's capital gains. The government will take 50% as a capital gain. "It's brutal," I explained. Continuing, I proposed an offer.

"You give us a 100% mortgage on your asking price. We won't insult you with a low-ball offer. This way, you only pay taxes on what you receive every year in mortgage payments, saving you $15,000 right off the bat."

Later, Alex told us he went straight home after our meeting and told his wife Betty, "I just met the cutest couple."

They accepted our offer. But it was far from being a done deal. I worked out on paper that the mortgage rate would have to be no higher than 7% for us to make payments and come out each month "cash positive." Alex went to his lawyer with the 7% and came back with a counter offer. "How about 6%?!" Wow, that was a gift. We all agreed. I contacted an attorney and set a closing date.

There was one more hurdle. We actually only had $54 in the bank. We had to borrow $1,500 to close. As luck would have it, I had been dealing with Chase since I was fifteen and they came to bat for us. Couldn't do that today after the S&L scandals and government in your face. Not to dwell on the negative, we were the proud owners of a mini shopping corner, and a wonderful Irish addition to our family, Betty and Alex Martin.

SHRUB OAK GALLERY

JEAN AND I WERE doing maintenance, painting the exterior of the second floor apartments, while standing on the Post Office roof. We paused for lunch, sitting on the roof looking across the parking lot at the house we now owned.

"What if we convert that house into a retail gallery and gift shop?", Jean said. I replied, "Okay, you run the gift gallery and I'll sell framing and artwork!" It took less than ten minutes to hatch a whole new career change.

Here we go again! We needed money, in addition to our 180% dedication, as well as a game plan. First, the money. I made an application at *The Patent Trader,* the local newspaper, as a pressman and they hired me straight away. Night shift!

Jean had another $1,500 left over from teaching ballet, so we figured the best place to go for gifts would be the New York Gift Show. Before any buying, we had to rebuild the house into a gallery. This would take a ton of money. First, if we rebuilt the second floor and attic, we could live in it with the business on the ground floor. Second, we would sell our Frank Lloyd Wright house.

What? Sell the house we planned to raise our children in? All those dreams would be dashed and for what? Another passionate challenge. It didn't take much; we were off and running.

I started the night shift at *The Patent Trader* in charge of a block long two-story web fed press that we printed three newspapers on: *The Patent Trader; Reporter Dispatch;* and *The Village Voice.*

I'd never seen this press before. *Rule #1:* Do not let anyone know you are terrified. *Rule #2:* Ask!

So I did.

"Hey, Frank," I called out, "where's the start button?"

"It's the green one," was all he said. Didn't need more, as all eight guys knew what their jobs were, once I had pushed the green button…"piece of cake."

Selling our Frank Lloyd Wright home was the next step. When we put it on the market, Jean cried for a full eight minutes.

"Okay, that's out of me," she said, "Let's get on with it!" The house went on the market for $50,000 and we sold it for $48,000 and thought we were the smartest people on the planet.

Don Lambo

SHRUB OAK GALLERY

The Shrub Oak Gallery was charming. The frame department took off. It was almost more than we could handle. The entrance off the front porch led you straight to an elongated work counter that was carpeted. My station was behind that counter with all the framing equipment needed to complete a customer's order, in-house. Turning left found you in a small but magical gallery, complete with a working fireplace. I built special shelving that hung from the ceiling with large chains. It was a place you really wanted to be in — comfortable, homey and packed with the latest pottery, jewelry, glassware and candles.

Our signature packaging was similar to the Tiffany Blue Box®. Ours was a white box with a shiny black lid that carried a sketch of our building, hot stamped in white. This was finished off with heavy twine.

It was expensive, but it put us on the map. Customers came in just to get the box with our logo on it.

We made many trips to the New York Gift Show in the City. Without fail, we came home with at least one outrageous item that sold for hundreds of dollars. Some we still have — a bronze tree sculpture and more than one original oil painting, which hang on our walls to this day. It was a very exciting, creative time and our collection of art and pottery is with us still as a reminder of those days.

I sold framing to the locals and made custom frames right there in the shop. Our business flourished, and I became an expert at blocking and stretching needlepoint, crewel, and cross-stitch. Our reputation for needleworks grew. I gave lectures to several women's clubs on what to do with their needlework after they had finished their projects. Of course, I included a vocal ditty and sometimes a soft-shoe to keep them awake. Business was booming.

We were blessed to have Jo Pasby as part of our growing family business. Jo, and her husband Brian, were parents of two young girls who took ballet lessons from Jean. They were steady and loyal in their support of Jean's classes.

One summer day, Jean got a call telling her the girls wouldn't be returning to fall classes as their purse strings needed to be tightened. Their participation in the ballet classes needed to end.

Jean didn't pause in her reply. "You have supported me these past years, now it's my turn. Just send the girls as usual and we won't ever speak of tuition again."

During the building stage of the Shrub Oak Gallery, I was in the Gallery gutting the walls when a bang came from the front door. I opened the door and there stood Jo and Brian. Although Jean had known them for years, I had never met them and had no idea why they were here. I invited them in and in the middle of all the rubble and chaos they told me what Jean had done for them when things were tough.

"We are here to pay you back!" It was indeed a genuine moment. Brian worked his butt off preparing the Gallery and Jo became Jean's right hand. Jo managed the shop and the Pasby family has become part of our family, still true to this day.

Matinee days, I wasn't behind the counter. With all that was happening with the business end of our lives, we were still dancing. So on any given Wednesday or Saturday, customers would come into the Gallery and ask for me. They would discover, "David is in the city today, he has a matinee."

Whoaaa, impressive. Very good for business. And so it went.

We thought we were busy then. We were invited to consider opening a second shop in the original Westchester Mall in Peekskill, NY. *Shrub Oak Gallery II* was born.

With Jo on board, we signed contracts and started building a new store. Jeanie was already selling David Yurman designer jewelry, so we kept some gift items but concentrated on the jewelry. Being in a mall is like no other experience. You are presented with a concrete slab and the rest is yours. Well almost — all yours with the union. Unlike building a business on property you own, the Mall was built by union members. And now our new gallery had to be built by union members.

The couple that ran the Shrub Oak Deli on our corner property informed us they had a buyer for their business. As written in their lease, they needed our approval of the prospective new buyers before the sale.

We told our tenants we would not approve a sale; but give us a number and we might be interested. They did, we did, and our lives got even more complicated. It was quite an adjustment for us to fully realize that we were the owners of a German deli.

Our schedule was a little hectic to say the least. I opened the Deli at five a.m., worked till ten, crossed the parking lot to open the Shrub Oak Gallery, sold framing till five, crossed back to help close the Deli by seven. Then dinner with Jean and our daughter Jennifer, heading off afterwards to the Gallery downstairs to make all the frames that were sold that day.

David, Jean, and Jennifer Ann Bean, 1966

~ 11 ~

Enter Jennifer

GUESS WHAT?

J EAN WAS TEACHING BALLET in our Shrub Oak home and received an offer from choreographer Bobby Herget. He asked her to be part of a cabaret in New York City. It was happening at the famed Lou Walters' *Latin Quarter* nightclub, founded by Barbara Walters' father. For Jeanie, this meant driving into the City with a challenging nightclub schedule, getting home at 2 or 3 a.m.

Doing cabaret would be a great experience, and so it was. After applying for her cabaret license, Jean started rehearsals in the role of a "pony"— one of the two girls, at five feet tall, who would be the very energetic advance dancers used to bring on the very tall showgirls.

Jean was wonderful and the show was a big success. Driving home alone at night was a concern; so I volunteered to drive her every night. But she declined the offer. Nevertheless, it didn't seem prudent to let Jean drive our Volkswagen Bug into the City and back home again alone at night.

Solving that problem proved to be quite easy. We simply put a dummy in the passenger seat. So, every night she trotted off with her dummy. In the morning, we would have tea and discuss the show and catch up on the events.

On one particular morning, Jean remarked, "Someone is changing out my shoes at the show. I'm sure they're playing games with me."

"What sort of games?" I asked.

"Every night, I get a different pair of shoes and they don't fit! I think one of the girls is trying to trip me up."

"They must be," she insisted. "My shoes simply don't fit. Surely my feet don't just grow overnight!"

Jean was convinced that someone was messing with her.

Then there was the throwing-up in the mornings. *What's that all about? What? Morning sickness? Could it be?*

One evening at dinner, Jean placed a box on my plate. It was a small box with a ribbon.

"What's this?" I asked.

"Just open it!" she said with a grin.

The lid came off and there were some very strange things inside. I was looking at an unfinished pair of tiny knitted socks, a silver bauble that looked like a rattle — and then the tell-tale item that turned on the light bulb for me: a bottle of aspirin. *Oh my God, she is going to have a baby.*

Jennifer

THE NEXT FEW MONTHS OF 1966 were exciting and happy. Cyril was thrilled and couldn't wait until July, Jean's expectant month. We commuted from Shrub Oak to the City to see Dr. Irving Saxe for checkups. Jean developed a passion for Dr. Brown's Celery soft drink and a hot pastrami sandwich with a kosher pickle. We never missed this deli treat on our trips to the doctor.

In July, we went in for a checkup, fully expecting and hoping to get an okay to admit Jean to the hospital. On the way down, we agreed that if Jean ended up not being admitted, we would go to the deli for our usual pastrami and Dr. Brown's. I dropped her off at Dr. Saxe's office for her appointment, and then went to park the car.

As I arrived back in his office, Dr. Saxe was coming out. "Hi, Mr. Bean, how would you like a pastrami sandwich?"

"Oh, what a shame. We were hoping to be admitted today," I replied.

"You are," he said. "You take Jean over to the Flower and Fifth Hospital and admit her. I'll finish up here, and you can pick me up and we'll go out for a pastrami sandwich."

Turns out he knew nothing of our agreement about the pastrami. After admitting Jean, I picked up Dr. Saxe and we went to Sardi's theatre restaurant on 44th Street for a nice meal. *Forget the pastrami!* I managed to get Dr. Saxe back to the hospital at about ten-thirty. Jean had been prepped and sent notes out to me in the waiting room signed "Baldy." She started labor at eleven o'clock and Jennifer made her appearance at 1:00 a.m., July 27, 1966. I waited till 6:00 a.m. before calling Cyril, knowing he would be up early for Mass.

The phone rang. "Hello." It was the sound of Cyril's voice.

"Hello, Grandpa," I blurted out. He hung up! I called him back.

"Why did you hang up? Jean just had a baby girl!"

"Oh how wonderful, dear boy! Was everything alright?"

"Perfect!" I responded. "Seeing that you just hung up on the mention of 'Grandpa,' what do you want to be called?"

"How about Cyril?"

"Well, would you approve of Uncle Cyril?"

"Yes, dear boy," he said with delight. "Uncle Cyril would be lovely."

Jennifer was born on the last Wednesday in July, and by that Sunday, we were in Ridgefield, Connecticut visiting "Uncle Cyril." Nearly every weekend we spent at Cyril's. "Lone Rock" was its official name, twenty-six acres with an upper and lower pond. We loved being there and Cyril loved having us.

From the moment we walked out of the hospital with our six-pound bundle of joy wrapped in swaddling clothes, Jennifer

Jean, Jennifer and Uncle Cyril

Jennifer and the "Perpetual Doll"

has given us a reason to rise out of bed every morning and tap dance. If ever there was an event in our lives that changed our world on a spectacular scale, birthing our daughter has never been topped.

From the get-go Jennifer was brought up as though we were developing a full-blown production in the play of life. We have never done anything by half, and this new show was about to be written day by day by two show folk parents who didn't know how to do it any other way.

Our quest was not to spoil Jennifer — and we agreed not to buy totally unnecessary toys with our hard-earned money. This was a practical decision, as our life's production had a limited budget and the simple fact was that everyone else in the world bought toys for the baby. We amused ourselves with Jennifer before she could walk by driving to a department store and allowing Jennifer to run up and down the aisle in a walker.

Then there was the "Perpetual Doll" — a stroke of genius by Jean, collaborating with a close neighbor friend in creating the special rag doll. They dressed her up in fancy clothes and a hat, and presented her to Jennifer as a present. Jennifer loved her doll and played with her for hours.

On those occasions when Jennifer would get bored playing with her doll, and Jean would find it on the floor being ignored, she would take the doll, wrap it in a gift box and put it away. It wouldn't be long before an occasion would present itself when Jennifer was deserving and out popped a beautifully wrapped gift box containing the "Perpetual Doll." One thing you must admit regarding Jean and me: we remain consistent. The last time Jennifer opened a beautifully wrapped box and discovered her familiar doll, she was over 50 years old. *We did laugh!*

JENNIFER'S PAYDAY

DURING the Shrub Oak Gallery years, Jennifer was growing fast and becoming a very thoughtful person. She would often sit on the carpeted work bench in the Gallery after school and read to me while I cut mats or made frames. She read the biography of Helen Keller, and since I had met her during the run on Broadway of *Peter Pan,* it took on special meaning.

At this time, Jennifer also began working in the shop. She would tidy up and help me maintain a clean environment — essential in light of all the artwork entrusted to our care. I paid young Jennifer and thus continued our family motto related to work. "If you are given a task or job, then the goal is to put 180% into that effort. No matter what it involves, 180% — and I guarantee success." This is something a dancer instinctively knows; no one else can take class for you. Your success is up to *you.*

This brought us to an ever so important element of the chosen work: payday. I would give her money for the task she was doing, like any father would. But I felt that there was something missing each time I gave her a couple of dollars. She took the money, stuck it in her pocket and went upstairs to do her homework. There was a reward for a job well done, but no goal. This is when we made a "deal" that every parent might consider when rearing their children.

"THE DEAL"

I F JENNIFER WOULD AGREE to give me back any amount of her earnings, I would match it and deposit it into a savings account in her name. A simple plan that comes with one proviso: You must promise never to spend this money in your lifetime! *Wow.* Now, what in the world does that mean? Simple. You must never spend the money. Move it around all you like, one investment to another, but you cannot spend it in your life-time!

She was only eight years old and had no clue to what she really agreed to. And so it started. We first opened an account at the bank and for every nickel she gave me from her earnings, I matched it. We soon had $100 which bought a CD (certificate of deposit) at a favorable interest rate.

By the time Jennifer was eleven years old, we were trading CDs at 16% interest. (In the '70s this was possible). Jennifer would go through the newspapers and find the best rates for CDs and we built a lovely port-folio. More often than not, she would give me all of the money she earned which, by my own rules, I had to match. It was an exciting game we played and her financial education blossomed.

Years later, she and her husband were in the market for a new home. It was shortly after they were married. Jennifer came to us and announced, "The penny just dropped! My money, I can't spend in my lifetime, right? But I can move the money to a house as an invest-ment."

She did indeed move her money into the new house and, of course, she has yet to spend it! It's a great plan. It teaches finance, responsibil-ity, and patience — all the attributes you want your kids to have.

THE FIREBIRD

ONE MEMORABLE DAY, Jennifer came to me with a plan. She had her eye on a new 1983 Pontiac Firebird. And she had it all figured out.

"I have plenty of money in my portfolio," she explained, "and we can buy the car outright with just $14,000. We won't have payments and we won't miss the money from my savings!"

As reasonable as it sounded — and I agreed it was a good idea — I said to Jennifer, "But you agreed not to spend it in your lifetime."

What now? Her body language spoke immediate disappointment.

"There's a different way you can do this," I said. "We'll call it the 'car plan.' As you're working, you can save up enough for a downpayment. Our deal still stands, and whatever you manage to save, your Mom and Dad will match. Once you buy the car, you can pay it off monthly from your paycheck."

It was a deal. It didn't take long, and her pitch-black Firebird found a spot in her young history — still spoken of fondly nearly forty years later. Of course, the tag line would read: "Would I love to have that car today!"

Jennifer and Jean in the Firebird

A Brief Visit in Boston

AS HER HIGH SCHOOL GRADUATION approached in 1984, Jennifer didn't know what she wanted to do next. She definitely didn't want to go to college simply to go to college. We had heard of the Katherine Gibbs School in Boston, which would give her a solid background in secretarial skills. The three of us took a drive to Boston to attend an open house at the School.

After checking into our hotel, we dined at the world famous Faneuil Hall. A real delight. Touring the Gibbs School the following morning, not so much. In 1984, the School appeared to be a finishing school for girls with an emphasis on deportment, white gloves and a regimented lifestyle totally void of fun and games.

It was apparent Jennifer was not having any of it, which perplexed her mother to no end when discussing it in the car all the way home the following day.

"Why wouldn't you want to go to such a charming school in the beautiful city of Boston? It would be divine!"

"Mother, mother, mother," Jennifer replied, "You are the one who wants to go there, not me! Maybe you should be the one to enroll."

There was a long pause and a very diminished "Oh" escaping from her mother. And that was that.

Jennifer's Graduation, 1984

Jennifer Bean, 1985

ALL HER BAGS WERE PACKED...

AFTER MAKING HER DECISION that the Katherine Gibbs Secretarial School in Boston was not the right match for her, Jennifer decided to look elsewhere. She was intrigued by a travel agent school in Florida; after much thought, she gleefully enrolled.

Mother and daughter had great fun shopping for clothes together, looking for just the right outfits for a budding travel agent being trained in Florida. Mom also helped prepare Jennifer for her first extended stay away from home.

With bags packed full of her clothing and all her favorite jewelry, Jennifer was ready to leave. She assured us that she would call once she had arrived safe and sound in the Sunshine State. With a hug and a kiss, we bid our grown daughter good-bye at the airport.

Jennifer's call came far too soon. We knew immediately that something was wrong. Her voice revealed her panic, as she babbled on and on, quite incoherently.

The flight was perfect she explained. But, after collecting her luggage, the "Red Cap" who had assisted her, didn't stop and deposit her luggage at the waiting bus. He took off into the crowd.

In a split second, the thief made off with her entire year's worth of everything. All too vividly, she learned her first lesson in what to instruct her client travelers: be aware and alert of those around you from the get-go!

Her career as a travel agent was short-lived. Jennifer did indeed complete her studies and became a certified travel agent. But she realized very soon that she simply could not sit in an office at a desk for eight hours. The confinement was not in compatible with her DNA.

Our daughter is our pride and joy without reserve. She is empowered with three ingredients required in life that make it possible to be anything and everything that she might want to be:

#1. Passion — it's the 180 Rule.

#2. Theatre — the ability to be and sell yourself — and loving the process, is the icing on the cake.

#3. Knowledge — the ability to count to 100 without relying on your cell phone.

These three elements are remarkably evident everyday in everything she does as our resident entrepreneur of Jeanie Bean & Family!

It's a Gas!

THERE ARE TIMES IN YOUR LIFE when it pays big dividends to be a Dad. Jennifer had scheduled an appointment with her doctor for a colonoscopy; she asked me to accompany her for moral support and to be that ultimate Dad and resident chauffeur.

The twenty-minute drive to the clinic was swift, with abundant chatter from me to divert her mind from the ultimate purpose of the journey: the dreaded colonoscopy. The goal: *Keep Calm and Carry On,* regardless.

Avoiding the sordid details of the procedure that took place that morning, I proceed now to the recovery room in which Jennifer was slowly coming around, reentering consciousness. The attending nurse kindly described the possible aftereffects that Jennifer might expect. The most likely effect: an abundance of gas, a normal post-colonoscopy occurrence.

It wasn't long before Jennifer transferred her attention to her growling tummy. And she left no doubt that her attention was focused on the hunger pains. Her first intelligent utterance, "I'm hungry, let's get out of here."

The ultimate reward after an early morning colonoscopy is breakfast. A lumberjack breakfast at that. We were off to claim her reward.

The parking lot was full, as was the Cracker Barrel Restaurant. We were ushered to a table within the crowded dining room and proceeded to order Jennifer's reward. Considering the hour-long procedure she had just undergone, she was looking quite fit, as the color began to reappear in her face. The breakfast arrived and Jennifer plowed into it like crows on roadkill. It was fun to watch.

We were a few minutes into the meal and I looked over to Jennifer and noticed she had stopped eating and her face was frozen, with her eyes nearly popping out of her head. Something was wrong and she managed to utter, "Uh oh, I gotta go." With that she quickly rose, moving her chair back as she stood up, and made a beeline to the ladies' room. Sitting there by myself, I thought, *must be the orange juice.*

It wasn't long before I saw her reappear, making her way to the table through the crowd. But this time, she had a twinkle in her eye — and a smirk on her face.

"You won't believe what just happened in there," she gushed. "I rushed into the ladies' room and found an empty cubicle. Dad, I created some noises in that cubicle that you might have thought was a reenactment of World War II."

"As I got myself back together," she recounted, "I opened the door and found this lady standing with her back to the sinks with a horrified look on her face. I didn't skip a beat, walked straight up to her and said, 'Don't have the Breakfast Special.' Then I walked out the door."

Ah . . . It's the simple things in life that cheer you up! We laughed all the way home.

Jennifer and me

THE TREASURE OF FAMILY

JENNIFER HAS BLESSED US with four grandchildren to die for. Bryce, now 27, is a Navy Corpsman who specializes as a surgical technician. She is now working for a Marine unit at Camp Pendleton in San Diego. While in Guam in 2017, she met Ralph, a fellow surgical technician. Early in 2019, Bryce reenlisted for three more years, and was stationed in California. In late 2019, she married Ralph. Their wedding took place compliments of the Navy while he was still in Guam and Bryce was in California. More than 4,000 miles apart, and yet they still managed to put on a show — in three different locations via FaceTime. Showbiz, it's in our blood.

As of this writing, Connor James is nineteen years old. Tall, handsome, and huggable. In 2020, in the middle of the Covid pandemic, he graduated from high school from the back of his dad's pickup truck. All of the students stayed in their cars with their families. When they arrived at the outdoor archway, they jumped out while wearing a mask, and were handed a diploma.

Jennifer went double duty with the arrival of Jake and Madison. At age 16, they are about to be high school juniors. Both of these kids are honor students and super sportsmen — Jake, a lacrosse goalie, and Madison, a devoted equestrian.

Our family is complete with our son-in-law James, a dedicated New York City firefighter. James is a decorated member of FDNY Rescue 1. The FDNY is the largest municipal Fire Department in the US and the second largest in the world, after the Tokyo Fire Department. Rescue 1 is one of five specialized rescue companies in the FDNY that requires special equipment and training. There isn't anything these firefighters can't do, and won't do, with passion. The 180 Rule comes to mind.

Nan

Papa

OUR TREASURE of SEVEN:

Jennifer

James

Bryce

Ralph

Connor

Madison

Jake

Jean & I in the early '80s

~ 12 ~

Glimpses of Life
After West Side Story

AUDITIONS

Driving into new york city for an audition was an event. Sometimes quite stressful. We did many auditions in the early '70s. We would sing our audition all the way into the City. I remember Jean had to sing *I Love A Cop* from *Fiorello,* standing in the middle of the office of theatre producer Jean Dalrymple. No music, just belting it out. It wasn't easy. Remember, we were dancers who sang, not singers who moved a little.

Reading auditions was tough. I had to go off with the script and memorize it quickly. Graduating high school I could read, but my comprehension was lacking. During the run of *West Side Story* in London, I realized how bad my reading was. My solution was to read aloud in bed every night. I read aloud *From Here to Eternity* and *The Agony and the Ecstasy.* What a time to have lived. My reading did improve and after *Lust for Life* there was no holding me back!

Today, I am asked on occasion to talk to the young people in high school about theatre and dancing. Without a doubt, playing an instrument or taking a dance class gives them a leg up in their world because they come away with discipline in their lives. No one else can practice for you. You have to knuckle down, take classes, and work your butt off to be any good. This profession is a world of *No thank-yous*, but with discipline and training you learn to handle the *Noes* in life, no matter what you are doing. For every fifty auditions you give, you might get one gig. In theatre, at that rate, you will be eating well.

TV COMMERCIALS

JEAN WAS CHOSEN to have a commercial built around her for a new toothpaste from Colgate called pHisoHex. "Young Broadway actress Jean Deeks uses pHisoHex," etc. Our agent had kept us busy with one audition after another in our quest for work.

On one particular day, I was sent off for another commercial. The drive into the city was usual; Jean went shopping for her Estée Lauder cologne while I kept my appointment. The director put me on camera and we simply started talking. No script, we just had a chat.

"This commercial we're shooting," he explained, "is based on a young actress being filmed on stage during a scene of a play."

"You," he continued, "would be in the scene on stage as her husband. But I'm thinking you don't really look like her husband!"

I perked up, "Is this the commercial with Jean Deeks?"

He looked surprised. "Yes, it is," he answered.

"Well, I *am* her husband!"

I got the job. The commercial ran for a few months and we did well.

I auditioned for an Edie Adams, Muriel cigar commercial. You might say I blew the competition out of the water.

Five guys were up for the commercial. As we lit and smoked a cigar, a voice-over would roll, informing the viewer how wonderful the cigar was. In our audition for the director, we were lined up and each given a cigar to light. Thanks to my fellow Jet, Bert Michaels, I wasn't a novice.

I took my time, rolled the cigar in my fingers next to my ear to appreciate the freshness, drew it across my face to savor the aroma, and then the clincher. I held the cigar out in front of me and rolled the end around the flame of a match before puffing it to life. This assures an even burn at the whole end of the cigar. I had to do it three more times. I was sporting a goatee at the time and they loved it. Again I got the gig.

Jean was also in the ad — as a square dancer in the background. In the foreground was Edie Adams, doing her famous, "For modern smoking pleasure and a taste that is sublime...why don't you pick one up and smoke it sometime?!"

During this scene, there was a segue cutting to me smoking a cigar. The director was nervous about my beard. Throughout the morning set-up, he kept suggesting that I might look younger without the beard. Eventually, he sent me off to make-up and they shaved my facial hair. Coming out of make-up, I overheard the producer call out for "the guy with the red beard." I still did the commercial, and Jeanie and I again were paid good money for old rope — *a piece of cake.*

Television Specials:

Dinah Shore, Perry Como and Leslie Uggams

WORKING ON BROADWAY was not a moneymaker. Bringing home $125 after taxes in the '60s and '70s was barely a working wage. Doing TV specials and commercials put us over the hump. The *Dinah Shore Show* was one of them and fun to do. For one particular show, Harry Belafonte was the guest star and the entire show was dedicated to the Peace Corps. Sargent Shriver (originator of the Peace Corps with JFK) made an appearance. The entire audience was made up of Peace Corps volunteers. Our dance numbers were very physical and exhausting. But the money was good.

The Perry Como specials were a snap. An easy day's work, but sometimes a bore. Perry Como was sooo laid back. So nonchalant. In rehearsals, he was ever so cool. He wore his overcoat at the run-throughs. Perry was a TV and recording artist with a voice that was soft and quiet. I'm sure he would never have been heard on the Broadway stage. Without a mike, he would never have had a career. His talent was as gentle as the sound he produced. Like Mary Martin, you wanted to hug him.

Jean was hired as a dancer on a Leslie Uggams TV special. My wife rarely talked about the experience, but it was another one of those money-for-old-rope gigs. When her check arrived in the mail, we went straight to the Ritz Thrift Shop on 57th Street and bought her two fur coats — a full length purple and grayish mink and a beaver jacket that was short to the waist. She looked gorgeous! I dare say she wore both of these coats completely out. *Thank you, Leslie Uggams!*

A SPECIAL SPECIAL:

The Dangerous Christmas of Little Red Riding Hood

A TELEVISION SPECIAL STARRING CYRIL as the Big Bad Wolf, Liza Minnelli as Little Red Riding Hood and Vic Damone as the Woodsman/Hero Hunter, *The Dangerous Christmas of Little Red Riding Hood* was a memorable 1965 broadcast.

The Animals singing group from England was Cyril's wolf pack. A fun cast. Lee Becker Theodore, from the original Broadway production of *West Side Story,* choreographed the show. The rehearsals were exciting. Lee was giving us some dance choreography that was very me. It was so easy and wonderful to dance. My comfort level with her work was a 10 — that is, until the costumes arrived.

I was a goat. My headdress was the tallest, largest thing I've ever worn — and impossible to dance in. All that wonderful movement Lee gave me was shot to hell by my big head and long tail. Goats don't even have a long tail…but I did! Perhaps I was a kangaroo.

Liza Minnelli was young and full of talent. Excited to be with dancers, she was fun to hang out with. I came away with the feeling she wanted to come home with us and be part of the family.

The music was written by Jule Styne. During rehearsals one day, we were on a five-minute break when I gave Jule a

Liza and the goat

memory test. *Did he remember ten years ago when he, Betty Comden, and Adolph Green introduced the Lost Boys in* Peter Pan *to the song* Wendy, *and this fourteen-year-old boy being asked which key he sang in?*

His eyes brightened and he sprang to a piano and sang *My Cutey's Due at Two-To-Two Today.* He remembered nearly the whole song. The wonder of Jule Styne was forever embedded in my mind. Here was a man who wrote *Gypsy* and many other show tunes, and now I saw firsthand how he was able to create as he did. His memory was like a steel trap. His brain seemed to be five miles ahead of the rest of the world. A fun experience I'll never forget.

Even though Cyril and I were in the same production together, our rehearsal schedules didn't match, and we didn't hang out much. When The Boss was working, it wasn't the time for small talk with him anyway. He was so laser-focused on his craft.

Singer Vic Damone was the Woodsman and for the rehearsals and taping of the show, he was the warbling woodsman!

THAT HAT: OFF-BROADWAY

OUR NEXT SHOW was *That Hat.* A musical version of the *Italian Straw Hat.* It starred Pierre Olaf, that perky Frenchman with whom we had worked in *Around the World in 80 Days.* He had made a big hit in the musical *Carnival,* for which he was nominated for a Tony Award as best supporting actor. Jean and I were the love interest and our dance number, "Tête-à-Tête," was designed to entertain and set the stage for the next scene. We would do wonderful lifts and then push a sofa onto the stage to set the next scene. It sounds awful, but it was fun and well-choreographed.

Our opening night was one to remember — or perhaps one to forget. Jean and I were on stage setting up the "Tête-à-Tête" dance number; the stagehand who was assigned to set up our furniture props in the wings was out having a cigarette. As a result, we had to improvise the entire dance number without the props. It was a disaster. One of those moments in life that was so embarrassing we simply wanted to hide. My skin crawls when I think of it! The phone rang the following day. I took the call on the terrace of our Shrub Oak home.

"Who was that?" Jean asked.

"We don't have to go in tonight," I shot back, "The show closed!" A one-nighter. Well, now we can plant our garden.

DANCING OUR WAY TO THE TONIGHT SHOW

THE DEMISE of our Off-Broadway flop in *That Hat* left us at in a stew. *What next?*

Ed McMahon was hosting a new television show called *Talent Scouts.* Famous celebrities would appear on his show and introduce an unknown talent they had discovered. Our celebrity was Cyril Ritchard. Introducing Jean and me as the newlyweds, he noted that we had met while performing in the London production of *West Side Story,* and he shared a bit of our history.

The dance number we had choreographed by Dania Krupska (*That Hat*) was indeed from *West Side Story* and a total flip-flop from the number's original premise. *America* was originally performed by Chita Rivera on Broadway as a Puerto Rican not wanting to return to Puerto Rico. Our premise was presenting *America* with an English accent, set in an American supermarket, with one of us not wanting to return to England. The number was charming.

Within a day or so of the telecast, we had several interesting inquiries. The agent for the world famous dance team Marge and Gower Champion offered to make us into the *next* world famous dance team. We turned down the opportunity simply because we didn't want to work the night club scene. My, how self-assured we were in the day!

To our surprise, the *Tonight Show with Jack Paar* booked us in to do the same number. Jack had left the show and the guest host that evening was my idol, Donald O'Connor, one of America's great hoofers. He starred with Gene Kelly in *Singin' in the Rain*. During the pre-broadcast rehearsal held on the afternoon of the telecast, we met Donald O'Connor but, alas, I did not get the chance to get acquainted.

FISHERS ISLAND:

A Summer in Never-Never Land

"ONCE YOU HAVE FOUND YOUR WAY THERE, you will never, never grow old." Peter Pan knew what he was about; for one lucky excursion, we found ourselves on Fishers Island, seven miles southeast of New London, CT. It too was magical — calling the Beans to another venture.

I'm sure Peter Pan was with us on the two-hour journey to New London in our maroon Mercury station wagon in the summer of 1975. The ferry ride was less than an hour, but I'm sure flying with a bit of fairy dust would have been easier on my stomach.

We had no idea where we were or where we were going on the island. Nine miles long and one mile wide, it didn't seem to matter. We could probably do the island, lunch someplace, and catch the three o'clock ferry back. The year-round population totals about 250 residences; we're talking small here.

We found ourselves in town and outside the office of the local real estate agency. Looking at all the rentals posted in the window, we found a house for rent with pictures and stuff. God knows how we booked it, but we were in Never-Never Land and we had a week's booking. (That's another way of saying I don't remember the details.) But we left Fishers Island that day excited to return for a week's vacation in July.

Our subsequent stay on the Island was wonderful and full of memories—fishing, lobsters, painting, and golf. During our stay, we got to know the local realtor. We must have looked at every house for sale on the island.

One such home was owned by a very prominent family. The estate was on the market for three million dollars. The realtor took us to see it. Located on the west side of the road, the house was not on the beach. The massive two-story shingled home had nine bedrooms, five baths, a fabulous kitchen, and a lanai that looked out to a lovely six-acre lake. The guest cottage had just undergone renovation at a princely sum of $80,000. A most beautiful estate for sure. It was typical of Jean and me to get ourselves involved, enjoying the fun ride.

The following day, our realtor called, telling us that "The Mrs." was on the island. He had told her all about us and it turned out that she would love to meet us. We agreed to meet at the house that afternoon. Jean prepared some delicious salmon and cucumber tea sandwiches — like the ones at our wedding reception — with a lovely bottle of wine, packed up in a picnic basket.

Our meeting was delightful and full of the latest skinny. It seemed that The Mrs. had been coming to the Island in the summer with her family for nearly thirty years. She and her husband had now divorced and that meant the sale of the estate. It was too sad really.

The day after our visit, our realtor called.

"The Mrs. was taken with you two and she wants you to have the house!"

"What does that mean? We couldn't afford a three million dollar mansion. What was she thinking?"

"She's willing to give you the house for the season — May through October — if you pay the utilities. She wants a vibrant, happy family who love the house, as her family has done for three decades. Our local town constable is living in the guest cottage and he will keep an eye on things if you're not there. It's a pretty nice offer!"

Indeed it was and, of course, we said, *Yes!*

Within a week, we were back on the Island. It didn't take long to fill the Island house with family and friends. My mother flew up from Atlanta and we were to pick her up at Kennedy Airport. As it happened, our guest-house constable was a pilot with a single engine four-seater airplane. We jokingly suggested he pick mother up and fly her here to the small airfield on Fishers Island.

"Sure", was his answer, "as long as you pay the landing fee at Kennedy." And so we did. Even better, Jennifer went with him as he taxied that tiny airplane up to a gate usually reserved for jumbo jets. Jennifer jumped out and ran into the terminal, found her grandma, and escorted her and her baggage out onto the tarmac where the tiny Piper airplane boldly awaited its passengers. Mother later confided the taxi ride to the runway was like a cartoon, a line of jumbo jets with this tiny speck patiently taxiing with the big boys.

Jean and I were standing by the runway waiting for them when they touched down on the Fishers Island airstrip. So began the summer of fantasy only Disney could invent.

Tracy Mann was a sister-friend to Jennifer, and spent a good deal of time on the Island with her. Their friendship is as deep today as it was forty years ago, even though each built separate lives with families and were ninety miles apart. Time disappears when they visit each other on rare get-togethers. It's a gift.

For that entire summer, I stayed home a few days at a time and ran the Gallery and the Deli. Jean would send our resident pilot to a small grass airfield in Putnam Valley (north of NYC), and he would fly me back to the Island. It was a super efficient one-hour flight, whereas the car and ferry took up to five hours, even when making good connections.

Our realtor appeared one afternoon with a message from The Mrs. After one of her luncheon visits with us, she had decided that we must be given the house permanently. She had had twenty-eight wonderful family years there and wanted the tradition to continue. She had instructed her attorneys to *give* us the estate. *A gift?* The estate was on the market for three million dollars.

As it happens, her attorneys objected and said she must sell us the house. Not, perhaps for three million, but certainly she could not gift us the property. "OK," she came back, "How about sixty thousand?" God knows where she got that number. So there we were, flabbergasted at the offer and not knowing how to react. Jean and I agreed this called for a business meeting. Every move we made was only after our number-crunching, soul-searching business meeting.

Our results were mind-blowing. We couldn't afford it! Do the numbers: The taxes were $30,000, maintenance $15,000, utilities $15,000. That's 60 grand and we hadn't considered the $60,000 that the lawyers wanted. We could receive the estate and create a consortium of investors to get through the expense, then sell the place for three million dollars. But that would defeat the heartfelt purpose of The Mrs. from the get-go. Not to mention being greedy and dishonest.

So there it was, our moral selves deciding to turn down this unbelievable gift. In the fall of 1975, we rented a U-Haul to clear out all the stuff that gathered during our fantastic summer on Fishers Island.

P.S. When I got my private pilot's license in the 1980s, I would fly to Fishers Island just for the fun of it. You find yourself in a daydream wondering, "What if…?"

My Piper "Cherokee" 180

FLYING: AN UNEXPECTED HOBBY

IN THE EARLY '80s, my friend John Lawrence, the landscape architect, arranged for me to meet him at the Dutchess County Airport. He was taking flying lessons. We could meet up and do lunch after his lesson. I was leaning on the wire fence at the airport waiting and watching the small planes fly in and out when one of these tiny planes pulled up close to the fence. The door swung open and out popped John.

"Hey, flyer," I greeted him, "Ready for lunch?" There was no pause in his reply. "I just got a call and I can't do lunch, but that guy in the airplane is waiting for you to take my lesson!"

"John," I said, "I didn't play with balsa wood planes as a kid. I really have no interest in flying! But thanks anyway."

"No, no," John insisted, "he really is waiting for you and I already paid for it!"

With that, John was off to his appointment. I could not believe I was about to climb into an airplane. I never in my life had a dream of piloting a plane. *God help us.*

The plane I climbed into was a Cessna 150 with barely enough room for the two of us. It truly made me think of the balsa wood toy planes. Although small, the plane had a million round dials and gadgets that would scare the pants off a monkey. The pilot fitted me with headsets to shut out the noise of the engine. Introductions took place and he immediately started talking to someone else not in the cockpit. "64667 Foxtrot, taxi active." "What in the world did he say?"

My earphones crackled again and another voice came on "667 Foxtrot, taxi bravo hold short at two four." The little plane sprang to life, and we were off, taxiing toward the runway. The end of the runway came up quickly and we were off with permission from the voice in my ears, as the plane was airborne.

"Pull back gently on the wheel," came the calm voice from the instructor sitting next to me. We must have been going sixty miles an hour and I did as instructed.

The world became a soft, floating sensation. "Right turn out approved," my earphones announced and it seemed just by looking in that direction the plane slowly made a right hand swing with its nose in the air, singing "I'm flying." We leveled out over Poughkeepsie, NY at about 3,000 feet, crossed over the Hudson River heading north/west. It was like nothing I'd ever experienced in my life. I felt secure and as one with our tiny airplane. I barely remember landing the Cessna 150, but I do remember the feeling of wanting to do it all over again. I was hooked!

I booked flying lessons and John and I enrolled in a ground school to learn the basics of flying and all the flight rules of which there are millions. The written test we had to pass was based on a set of 900 questions you could be given. You had no idea which of the 900 you would get, but rest assured, you must be prepared to know them all. It was ironic that you could actually pass your written exam with a score of 75%. Well, who in their right mind would fly with someone who only knows 75% of what he should?!

John and I were lucky. A friend of John's had a beautiful Cessna 172 that was mint and needed to be flown. It had four seats (unlike the two-seat Cessna 150). We could all fly the lesson and then stop for lunch somewhere. This is where the phrase "$100 hamburger" originated.

After a few months, we purchased a Piper Cherokee 180. The owner had passed away and the family wanted to sell the plane quickly. 7436 Whiskey was the call number on the 1963 Piper Cherokee. She was a low-wing beauty that flew like a baby. Her electronics were far from up-to-date. No GPS. We flew by charts and the guidance system called VOR. (VHF Omnidirectional Range). Tune in a radio frequency and fly to it; as you flew over the VOR, a little red flag would flip, indicating it was time to change the radio frequency to the next VOR.

You always studied the charts before every long flight. By making notes on the charts, you always knew where you were. As long as you did your homework, flying was stress-free and fun. Identifying rivers, buildings, towers, highways, and race tracks as you flew over them on route to your next airport was a challenge. I always knew where I was.

There was one exception though: my flight to Atlanta via Peoria, Illinois. The plan was to leave Poughkeepsie and fly to Peoria to pick up my brother Don. Then refuel and head for Atlanta to visit Mother. That was the plan. Heading west to Peoria, I ran into a snowstorm and was forced to land at a small airfield in Portland, Indiana.

My license allowed me to fly VFR only (Visual Flight Rules). I'm not allowed to fly through clouds or into a storm which requires an IFR rating (Instrument Flight Rules). A young chap at the Portland airport was a great help giving me info on where to stay and the best place to eat. He even threw me a set of keys to a new Volvo belonging to a fellow pilot who was off somewhere in his airplane. The hospitality was like instant family. I returned in the a.m. to find my Cherokee was refueled and cleared of the snow from the night before. Weather charts were printed out and I was ready to go without lifting a finger. The storm had passed, the sun was out, and I had a clear shot to Peoria from Portland.

It's wonderful flying the Midwest. All the roads go north and south or east and west. On my chart there was a road going west straight to

Peoria. This time I would fly a different kind of IFR: *I Fly Roads.* Thirty miles out, I contacted Peoria International to let them know who I was and that my intent was to fly into Mount Hawley Airport.

"36 Whiskey," I heard. " just follow that road you are following and Hawley will be at twelve o'clock as you cross the river."

"Thanks for the heads up," was my reply. I signed off and switched frequency to Hawley Airport.

Seeing my brother is always a kick. Don is a big man, six-foot-three, and definitely filling out all the clothing he wears. Not fat, just a big fun guy with a wonderful laugh. We buckled up in the Cherokee and headed south to Atlanta. Don spent most of his adult life in Illinois raising a family and selling grain silos to farmers. He knew the territory. Shouting over the engine noise through our headphones, I'd ask him, "Where are we, Don?"

"Let's see, fly down to that silo and, OK, yes, we're at so-and-so county. I sold that silo to that farm."

We landed in Bowling Green, Kentucky for lunch. The weather was glorious and it wasn't long before we were pointing the nose towards Atlanta. As we flew over Chattanooga, Tennessee, I called Atlanta ATC (Air Traffic Control) to request flight following — a service they provide to keep track of you and keep you on track to your destination.

"36 Whiskey, are you at 3,500 feet?" the voice on my earphones asked.

"Atlanta, no, I'm at 7,000 feet."

"36 Whiskey, it seems that your altitude encoder is inoperable. We are extremely busy, and without your altitude, flight following is denied. Have a nice day."

Wow, I just got thrown out of their airspace so to speak. I was shocked. I asked my brother, "If we stay on this heading, we'll fly straight into Atlanta. Would you recognize Lake Lanier when we fly over it?" (The lake is 50 miles northeast of Atlanta.)

His reply was reassuring, "I know that territory like the back of my hand. I got your back." So we pointed 36 Whiskey to our Atlanta heading and continued our conversation without thinking much about our course.

We never did see Lake Lanier, and the sun was rapidly going down in the west. *I think we're lost.* I had no idea where we were. It was a crushing blow to my ego. Lost? I don't get lost, I always know where I am. Nothing looked familiar on the ground and a touch of panic was setting in. I'd just have to swallow my pride and follow my training: The three C's — *Climb, Call,* and *Confess.*

Altitude is your friend in an airplane. So *climb* — and *call* the nearest ATC for help, while *confessing* you are lost! They will track you on a special frequency and lead you to an airport. I had no choice, I simply had to...

"Don, is that a beacon light down there?" I flew over a small airfield that seemed totally void of people and airplanes. I had no idea the field radio frequency, so I just flew downwind. It was spooky. Not a soul was visible and, as I turned final to land, the runway lights went on. Not a living soul to be seen. If you know the airport frequency, you enter it and click it three or four times and if they have lights, they will pop on. *How did the runway lights turn on?*

We had no idea where we were, let alone have a radio frequency for this airstrip. I taxied the plane to the row of hangers off the runway and spotted a phone booth at the end of the building. Don jumped out of the plane to find a sign that could enlighten us as to our where-abouts. No luck. He did find a sign in the phone booth that read, "Need a place to stay? Call Jim's B&B," with a phone number. Twenty minutes later, Jim arrived and transported us to a charming B&B where we had dinner with his entire family. An evening of delight does not go un-punished...Don snores like a sawmill in full operation.

There was a reason for getting lost of course. Don and I were having a great time heading to Atlanta and I did not calculate a slight crosswind; and although our indicated heading was correct, we were pushed north just over the border of South Carolina. The following morning we followed I-85 straight into Gwinnett County Airport. We were 80 miles off course, I confess.

How those lights came on is still a mystery to this day.

LAKE GEORGE

WHENEVER WE TRAVEL, Jeanie and I pick up the local real estate booklets. I was thumbing through one of these when I found a listing for property in Lake George, NY, about two hours north of Clinton Corners. "Look at this," I said, handing the booklet to Jean. "Five separate rental units, and a large three bedroom home with a kidney-shaped swimming pool. We should check this out."

Water sports, parasailing, fishing and camping are all alive and well on this magnificent thirty-two mile, glacial lake. Multimillion-dollar homes along its shores abound, as you travel north on the steamboat *Minne-Ha-Ha* to gaze at the haves, by the mostly wannabes. We contacted the real estate agent and made an appointment to view the property. And, you guessed it, we ended up purchasing it.

Lake George is a summer event for sure. Summer rentals are the backbone of commerce, providing high income for the high season. In the Village, you can buy T-shirts with clever sayings, trinkets of all kinds for the souvenir hunters, with food and coffee bars everywhere. Hotels and motels accommodate the thousands of tourists who flock to the lake described by Thomas Jefferson as "without comparison the most beautiful water I ever saw."

With Lake George being a summer vacation spot, we rented the house by the week at a very hefty rate for the twelve weeks of summer. Since Adirondack Community College was nearby, our granddaughter Bryce asked us if she could live in our house in Lake George while attending ACC. Bryce wanted to attend their well-regarded nursing program.

"Of course you can live in the Lake house," we said, "provided we can come live with you." Which is exactly what we did. It was the best time ever, especially for the girls. Nan and her granddaughter Bryce have a beautiful bond that money just can't buy.

Having fun in Lake George: Connor, Jake,
James, Madison, and Jennifer

Bryce in
Lake George

It seems that the apple doesn't fall far
from the tree... Theatre clearly runs in
their blood, as grandchildren Madison,
Connor, and Jake enjoy hamming it up.

185

BRAVO FOR
THE CHILDREN

THEATRE HAS ALWAYS PLAYED an enormous part of the life that Jean and I have led, on both sides of the pond. One year, we took on a full-blown bar and restaurant called the Union Jack Pub. Jean created a menu to rival any English Pub.

It was here in the Pub, while working the crowd, that I met a local school teacher who knew of our theatre background, particularly *West Side Story.*

"My eighth grade orchestra," she told me, "just completed and performed a suite from Bernstein's *West Side Story.* Would you like to hear them perform?"

My reply was instant and full of excitement, prompting her to schedule an early morning performance date at the middle school auditorium.

It was cold that morning and, finding myself to be the only soul in the large school auditorium, I didn't bother to remove my coat. If nothing else, it would serve to stave off the morning chill. Soon enough, I was warmed by the sight of 40 thirteen-year-old students taking the stage, clearly focused on tuning up their instruments.

What happened next was spectacular.

West Side Story filled the auditorium with the fabulous music of Leonard Bernstein. It was a sound I knew so well. And on this day, it was being played by a younger generation with such emotion and skill — right here in the Mid-Hudson Valley. I found it so inspiring to witness these young musicians playing one of the most challenging scores ever played on Broadway.

And the best was yet to come: the teacher-director invited me to join her on stage to speak with the students. How excited I was to have the opportunity to convey to them the gift that they had truly given to themselves and others through their hard work.

"This performance didn't just happen. You all worked for it and in doing so you gave yourselves a gift that will be with you forever. The gift of discipline. There isn't a thing in your lives ahead of you that won't be affected by the discipline you already practice now. I didn't do scales for you. *You* did it."

I recounted that, as a thirteen-year-old, I loved to tap dance — spending hours on one foot, doing a simple shuffle until I could create the tone and quality of that shuffle without thinking.

"You've done that! You know how! The discipline you've achieved will be there for you the rest of your life. Discipline will help you on your life's journey and it will be automatic. I can't tell you how thrilling it was for me to sit out there and soak in your efforts and talent, knowing how hard you worked to do this. Leonard Bernstein would have jumped up on this stage and hugged each and every one of you for the performance you just gave."

"Before I leave, I have a request of you. As you exit this stage, please give your teacher a hug. What she is giving you is priceless."

Cyril Ritchard

~ 13 ~

Cyril's Final Curtain Call

I N THE FALL OF 1977, Cyril was in Chicago with the musical *Side by Side by Sondheim,* and not sounding all that perky. I made a snap decision to take Jean and Jennifer (then 11) to visit Uncle Cyril in the Windy City. Cyril was delighted and I booked the two-hour flight to Chicago. We would stay with Cyril at the Ritz for the week before Thanksgiving.

Watching young Jennifer stroll into the Ritz brought instant memories of the book *Eloise at the Plaza* by Kay Thompson. This was to be a super fun time, and a chance for The Boss to have family to fret over as a doting father. We were swept into our hotel suite, unpacked and had lunch. Knowing that we were to see *Side by Side* the following evening, we found and booked the girls into a Vidal Sassoon Salon.

As usual, The Boss was very much in command and wonderfully interested in our business. While the girls had their hair appointment, I sat with Cyril and we went over his bills and caught up on the paperwork.

After our family met back at the hotel, the telephone rang and I heard a familiar voice saying, "Oh, hello dahling!" It was Mary Martin. She happened to be in the hotel a couple of floors above us. Mary and British actor Anthony Quayle were in Chicago with their two-character play *Do You Turn Somersaults?* We were all invited to Mary's suite for tea, with an invite to see *Somersaults* that evening.

189

We dressed, headed upstairs, and knocked on the door of Mary's suite. She appeared at the door and instantly it was old home week. After lots of shouting and hugs, Mary sat down next to Jennifer and opened a scrapbook. Pointing to a photo she said, "That is a picture of your dad when he was your age!" Imagine, this woman was on tour and she had brought a scrapbook with her! Mary Martin is credited with the one-liner, "There is a world of communication which is not dependent on words." This was one of those moments.

Our trip backstage after the show was memorable. Joining us, in all her splendor, was Carol Channing and her husband Charles Lowe. Seeing Jennifer standing next to Ms. Channing in her full-length white mink coat was a picture I will have in my head forever. Boy, that woman was tall, and exactly the same in person as we all knew her on stage. Ms. Channing related to us the tale of the white mink coat. It seems that the coat was stolen from her hotel room while she was performing in New Orleans. The Mayor of the city was notified and, story has it, he put out a directive that he wanted that white mink back within 24 hours. Ms. Channing got it!

We all huddled in Mary's dressing room and sang *Happy Birthday* to both Cyril and Mary. Both enjoy the same December 1st birthday. Even though we were a week early, it was certainly fortuitous that we paused to celebrate early.

The evening was special and we all went to sleep that night trying to remember all the delicious details of an extraordinary evening. Our wonderful week with The Boss was soon up and we reluctantly packed up our suitcases and headed for O'Hare.

Our life returned to normal back in Shrub Oak. With Thanksgiving upon us, we were entering a hectic season in the Deli — not to mention prepping for the Christmas rush in our Galleries.

On November 26, two days after Thanksgiving, I got a call from Cyril's longtime gentleman's dresser, Eric Harrison. The Boss had suffered a serious heart attack during a performance in Chicago. Within hours, I was at his bedside at Northeastern Memorial Hospital. He had indeed suffered a massive heart attack and was in a coma. A spokesman for the hospital described his condition as "extremely unstable."

The attentive medical staff was world class. He couldn't have been in better hands. Harrison brought me up to speed on the details of Cyril's collapse during the show. It was a matinee performance. Near the end of the play, with his work done, Cyril was quietly seated behind the audience. An usher discovered him slumped over. And, as it turned out, the head of cardiac surgery at Northeastern Memorial was in the audience. He immediately attended to the ailing star and rode with him in the ambulance to the hospital. Cyril couldn't have arranged for a better attendant. *Optimum Semper,* only the best.

Even though he remained in a coma, I spent day after day at his bedside talking to him. In the hope of keeping the atmosphere in his room positive and up-beat, I sang many of the songs that Cyril had recorded over the years. As the days wore on, I put together a list of his closest friends, calling them nearly everyday with a progress report. Among those most cherished to him were Mary Martin, Alfred Hitchcock, and Roddy McDowell.

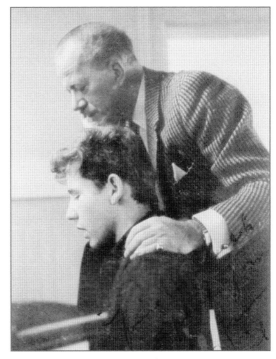

Cyril and David at the piano, 1956

Throughout this long, three-week vigil, there was a continual flow of best wishes and kind regards arriving from all over the world for a truly beloved man. And the atmosphere in the hospital never seemed to flag — in spirit and heartfelt concern.

On the morning of December 18th, Cyril died without regaining consciousness at the age of 79. His funeral was held at St. Mary's Church, near his cherished country home in Ridgefield, CT. Bishop Fulton J. Sheen, his friend and mentor, offered the funeral Mass. The Boss would surely have approved.

Cyril is buried at St. Mary's Cemetery next to his beloved wife of nearly twenty years, Madge Elliott. Their tombstone includes not only their given names, but also the name "Captain Hook."

For nearly a quarter century, Cyril was a very influential part of my life. Born halfway across the world, and more than forty years my senior, who would have ever imagined that this Aussie luminary, Cyril Ritchard, would end up being a father figure and friend for most of my life…and the best man at my wedding.

~ 14 ~

Moving North: Another Life

J EAN AND I continue to have a curious fascination with real estate. We did the tourist bit early in our marriage, now we travel and scout houses, as well as business and farm properties. It's great fun.

Every few months, I would take Jean for a long drive in the country. From Westchester County, we headed north on the Taconic State Parkway to get the cobwebs out. Eventually, you get familiar with the landscape and this day I had promised to stop at a local real estate office just off the Parkway with a wonderful name: Guernsey Real Estate. The name reminded us of something we loved — the Guernsey brown cows. The name made us smile. On a sunny fall day in 1978, I pulled into the parking lot and, before getting out of the car, we decided it best to establish a few rules.

First, we don't have much cash, so Rule #1: *Don't lead them on.* Rule #2: *We're just looking.* Rule #3: *Find out what's available and at what price range.* That's it! All set. Simple, nothing fancy.

"May I help you?" was the first friendly voice we heard as we entered the office, an old converted house.

"Yes, we're interested in a small getaway up here in the country. You know, something tiny!"

"My name is Gordon Hammersley." Nice chap, very tall, pleasant voice.

"Tell me exactly what you need and we will go from there," he continued.

"Well," I said, "something simple, ten acres, maybe a view, water would be lovely, a small house where we could spend weekends."

"And," Mr. Hammersley said as he focused our conversation, "how much do you intend to spend on your getaway?"

"About $30,000," I said with a straight face.

There was dead silence.

"Well, yes," Mr. Hammersley chimed in to fill the obvious gap.

"I tell you what, let me drive you about and look at the properties we have available and give you an introduction to the area."

Great idea. We left the office, and our tour of Clinton Corners began. We headed north on the Taconic State Parkway and immediately Gordon (we're already best of friends!) pointed to a hill off the Parkway.

Drawing our attention to a field on the left of the Parkway, Gordon said, "That property has a lovely view with a small house at the end of a half-mile drive, all uphill. Must be wicked in the winter. It's 42 acres and just sold, so I can't take you up there."

We drove on and saw a home in a hillside development that had an indoor pool. A two-acre lot with a $100,000 price tag. Heading southeast, Gordon again called our attention to a hill and said, "That's the other side of the 42 acres with the long drive. Can't imagine how they manage that driveway."

We continued on to the neighboring town of Stanfordville. After an hour of popping in and out of homes, we found ourselves back in the center of Clinton Corners, consisting of a large two-story building with a grocery store and deli. There was a horse trough in the middle of the square. We stopped for lunch, enjoying the charming country store.

"That's about it," declared Gordon. "If we get any new listings, I'll give you a call and you can drive up and get those cobwebs out," he said with a grin.

As we left the hamlet of Clinton Corners to get back onto the Taconic, Gordon drove slowly.

"On the right is the entrance to the property with the long driveway. Too bad it sold."

We pressed on. The day had been perfect. All the cobwebs were gone, and Jean and I had had a great day out, viewing some lovely (expensive) homes and arriving back home in Shrub Oak very refreshed.

We were about our business the following day when we received a surprise telephone call from our newfound friend Gordon Hammersley at Guernsey Real Estate.

"What's up?" I asked.

"You know that 42-acre property we passed several times yesterday? The one with the outrageous driveway?"

Successfully piquing our interest, Gordon continued.

"Well, the sale fell through and I thought it would be interesting for you to have a look. It really does have a great view."

After the 45-minute drive from Shrub Oak to Clinton Corners, we met Gordon and loaded ourselves into his car for the trek up the half-mile driveway.

We were halfway up the hill, and I exclaimed, "Stop the car!"

We stepped out in the middle of the hayfield on the hill. The views were unbelievable. We could see all the way south to Beacon, NY. On a clear day, we were told, one could see New York City. There we were, standing in the middle of the hayfield stunned by what we were viewing. I took out my checkbook, wrote a two hundred dollar check, and gave it to our friend Gordon. "This is our binder," I said. "Now let's go look at the house!"

OUR NEW HOME: BEAN HILL

T O SAY THAT we are an impulsive pair might be an understatement. The hill property, we later learned, was a bank repossession.

It was spring of 1979 when we closed on our new home, which we named Bean Hill. The dirt driveway up the hill wasn't a factor. Of course, it was approaching summertime. The house was a small ranch right on top of the hill. Views to die for. We could see all the way up the Berkshire Mountains to the north, and the views to the south were spectacular as well. There were no stands of trees on the property, as the fields had been cleared for hay.

Our first project was to install a swimming pool. Jennifer was going into the seventh grade and, except for work, there was nothing for recreation. We went to Herman's Nursery and inquired about a pool. Bill Herman sent us his new landscape architect, John Lawrence, fresh out of Syracuse University, to scope out the pool site.

Jennifer and her mother spent most of the summer at Bean Hill, and it was Jennifer who suggested we move there permanently. She had met some of the local kids in Clinton Corners and would be able to attend Millbrook Middle School with them.

But first there was an agreement Jennifer had to approve. If she went to school in Millbrook, she had to walk down the half-mile drive to catch the bus. Mom wasn't going to drive her every morning. Jennifer agreed!

Dad would make the 45-mile commute to Shrub Oak everyday. I brought up a box of shoes for the girls and we were moved in. *Done!*

There were mornings when Jean and Starfire (our pet goat) would accompany Jennifer down to the bus. Life was good. Jennifer got into the country life with gusto. She joined the 4-H and we bought a few sheep. They belonged to Jennifer and were her responsibility. Eventually, she showed them at the Dutchess County Fair in Rhinebeck.

CLINTON CORNERS COUNTRY STORE

IN THE FALL OF OUR FIRST YEAR in Clinton Corners, Jean learned that the local country store (the same place we had enjoyed lunch with Gordon) was on the market. The owners wanted to sell the business and the property. Above the store were apartments and next door was an attached house. This was a very local business. The interior of the store was all beautiful pressed tin. The walls and ceiling were in original 1908 condition. The equipment, on the other hand, was old and barely running. There were six compressors working very hard to keep the beer cold and the deli meat from spoiling.

To be sure, this building needed a lot of fixing. By December, we had agreed on a price for the entire lot, buildings, store equipment and inventory. We closed on December 29th, Jean's birthday. Had she known that the gift of this new adventure would put her to work for the next forty years, she may have had second thoughts. And so it began. We opened the Clinton Corners Country Store on January 1, 1980.

From the very first day, we loved the store. What a challenge. Jean was in charge of the food and grocery end of the business. I was the builder, accountant, and front man on the counter. The first week of business we suffered a rain storm with the winds howling. It was terrifying. In the middle of the storm, we heard a crash…more like an explosion. The walk-in cooler was built out over the basement freezer. An abandoned chimney that extended fourteen feet above the building had been blown over onto the roof of the cooler. The spine of the roof was broken, sending the entire cooler into the basement freezer.

We gutted the walk-in freezer and rebuilt a kitchen in the space where the walk-in cooler was. Across the entire back of the store we installed a 30' by 10' deep cooler/freezer. It had fourteen doors: four for the freezer and ten for the cooler. This eliminated the old worn-out compressors and a possible fire in the building.

"Mr. Bean" behind the counter

The Taconic State Parkway was only a half mile west of the store, but the internet wasn't yet guiding travelers our way off the Taconic. So we relied on our community for survival. We inherited a customer charge account system. Most families in the community had a charge book in a box under the counter. Customers would hold up a loaf of bread as they walked by the counter and out the door. I would write the amount in their monthly charge books. At the end of the month, I added their charges and handed them an envelope with a total amount due. Kids thought we were very special because everything was free. "Just hold it up for Mr. Bean to see it—and then walk out the door."

The children all held a special place in the store. They were magic. Truly, they were magic. I would make a very big deal out of finding a Tootsie Roll in each child's ear. Magic? It was more than that! The expression of disbelief on their faces was priceless. They never forgot it, and I found one in their ear every time they were in the store.

Decades later, I have reconnected with fully grown men in their 50s telling me appreciatively, in a very deep voice, "Mr. Bean, you pulled Tootsie Rolls out of my ear when I was a boy." Seriously, I had more enjoyment from the magic than they did.

Our children in the community all knew how to count their change. It was an easy education and a lot of fun. When a child bought an item they would automatically hand me the money for the purchase. I would hand them their change and knowingly palm some of the change. They would take the change and head for the door at which point I would call them back. "Did you get the right change?" I would ask. With a puzzled look, they would proceed to subtract the change in their hand. Lesson one, you add your change. The cost of the item, plus what I gave you as change equals the amount you gave me to pay for the item. Simple…and they learned quickly; I heard one child say to his friend, "Count your change, or Mr. Bean will rip you off if you don't!"

The holidays were special in the store. At Halloween, we encouraged the kids to come in with their costumes for a photo, which we would post during the week. We also gave out a half-dozen eggs to each of the kids for free. *Free,* but with rules. Rule #1: No throwing an egg at anyone who doesn't want an egg thrown at them. Rule #2: If you hit a car or building by accident, you must clean up the mess. (We had four five-gallon pails of water on the porch.) Rule #3: You must report back the next day and help clean up the eggshells. It was what we called "controlled violence." They had a ball and the porch was a mess for the day, but no one got hurt.

At Christmastime, Jean put up a tree in the window and set up a table with tons of stuff for making Christmas tree ornaments. Each of the children would make an ornament for the tree and sign it. They were allowed to help themselves to soda in the back cooler and Jean provided a table of snacks to munch on.

One day, the older boys disappeared, walking off with a six-pack from the back cooler, taking it out the back door. The next day, Jean, having witnessed the heist, called the boys together and then put on a tear-jerking drama, worthy of an Oscar. At the end of the performance she doled out the punishment: to meet the following day and clean the creek that goes through the town park. *Lesson learned.*

Jean and I were considering an addition of fresh-baked bread for our store and had a rep from an oven company come in to pitch a complete oven-to-counter system. We were very impressed with his presentation, buying the entire system — racks, trays, ovens, the lot. Here we go girls — a new career. Fresh croissants and pastries every morning meant getting up at 4 a.m. Word spread about our homemade bread and soon our business was booming. I got in early and set up the breads for proofing (rising a final time before baking) while the ovens were heating up. I'd put the coffee on first thing and customers would begin arriving early. Busy in the kitchen, I could hear the customers cashing themselves out on the register. Our customer base was family, we made it their store. It was a beautiful time. Jean was a whiz in the kitchen. Her breads were fantastic. Meat, breads and calzones to die for.

JEANIE BEAN & COMPANY

BY CHANCE, I found an English food importing company that sold "Paxo, Sage & Onion Stuffing." Very British. An item Jean grew up with. "Mum always 'ad 'er Paxo." I ordered a case and when it arrived, I marked it and placed it on the grocery shelf in the store. It wasn't but a week or two later when Jean called and asked me to bring home a box of Paxo off the shelf. I made a note for later, but when I went to the shelf, it was all gone. *Ta–da!* If Paxo sold in our store, what about other English food products? Jeanie Bean & Company, Inc. was born. Surely, if there is a nest of Anglophiles here in Dutchess County, what about all the Brits scattered about the rest of the country?

Jean and I put our heads together and made a list of typical British items you might find in an average British larder. Candy was on top of the list; tea and biscuits were next. But first we had to research the art of importing goods to the US.

We planned a trip to London and soon found ourselves having lunch in a pub with our shipping liaison, Barbara. Our purchased goods would be forwarded to her warehouse and loaded into our personal shipping container. Barbara was a wealth of knowledge — leading us to Booker Wholesale, where we bought all our groceries. She also gave us leads to wholesale dealers in pottery, china, flags, Christmas crackers, you name it, she had the contacts. It was so exciting.

A plus for us was the family visit. We stayed with Jean's parents and saw all the old friends we worked with doing *West Side Story* in London.

This was only the beginning. We still had to create a catalog and find space to do all this packing and shipping. The basement at our Country Store had a nine foot ceiling and 2,500 feet of space. We carpeted the old walk-in freezer and set up an office to process orders.

We decided to shoot our own photos for the catalog. I bought a book on "how to develop film" and purchased the equipment to develop my own. I borrowed an enlarger and essentially set up a photo shop in house. We found a printer for the catalog and we were set. Our first catalog held over 300 specialty items that we thought would make any heart skip

a beat when presented to an Anglophile living in the US. A British newspaper, the Union Jack, sold us our first mailing list. Our first mailing was 15,000 catalogs. We were in business. Our mailing was in summer and Jennifer was our phone order girl. Most orders came in the mail direct from the catalog, but the phone was essential for reorders and Jennifer was brilliant! Our customers would send her photos which soon covered our office walls. It too became a family business that

Jeanie Bean
& Company

seemed personal to customers and to our staff. Jeanie Bean's was the go-to place for all your British fare. We even produced our own line of tea. The orders poured in.

A slew of the local kids worked for us, picking, wrapping and packing. Christmastime was super busy. We brought Jean's Mum and Dad over from London and they worked their tails off in our new venture.

There is an epitaph to Jeanie Bean & Company. Our government decided that every food product sold in the US had to carry a label of nutritional value. Well, the Brits didn't! Every food item we sold we were allowed to add a printed nutritional value label before shipping. Imagine calling Cadbury's and asking them to divulge the nutritional value of any of their products. *Take a hike* was their usual answer and we did ask! We had to have all the food items analyzed here in the US, giving us the data required by the US FDA regarding the nutritional value.

Up until January 31, 1994, we could bring containers of products and apply our own labels of nutritional value. As of January 1, 1995, we had to send the labels to England and hire personnel to adhere said labels before being shipped to the US. Well folks, we were out of business.

Several years later the EU was in place and the EU adapted the US FDA regulations on nutritional values. All food products shipped to the US from Britain now conform; but it was too late for us and we shut down the company.

BEAN HILL FARM

MEANWHILE, BACK AT THE RANCH. Bean Hill was to become a real farm. A labor of love — with an emphasis on the labor.

Enter Pete Juerss, a twenty-one-year-old budding farmer. Pete owned all the equipment necessary for baling hay. Our fields needed mowing and Pete kept the hay fields pristine while selling the hay for profit. Since we had no animals to feed, it was agreed that Pete would maintain the fields for the hay.

The four sheep we had bought for Jennifer to raise and look after needed a place to shelter and sleep. This meant building a shed for them with some sort of fenced area. So, I built a lean-to off the side of the hill in front of the house, south of the pool. Sitting on our back deck overlooking the pool, we could keep an eye on the sheep.

Our first piece of equipment was Pete's old British (so apropos) Leyland tractor. It came with a sickle bar side mower and of course had a PTO (power take-off) on the rear to power a brush hog. One of the joys in life is to sit on a tractor and brush hog the perimeter of the hay fields while breathing in the fresh air and thinking of nothing. It was a time to sit on that little blue tractor singing *Oh, What a Beautiful Morning* from *Oklahoma* at the top of your lungs. A family of resident foxes would scurry into their den as I approached.

We bought an old 1957 Ford dump truck for $500. We called it Igor. This was the "go-to" truck. Before we had hay wagons, we threw freshly baled hay up on to the truck. Boy, we were healthy. Igor played a pivotal part on the farm, hauling everything. We even had our own brush dump on the property to handle the land clearing.

We got wind of an old barn on Schoolhouse Road that the owners wanted removed. Pete and I drove Igor to have a look. It was a two-story, 15' x 20' barn with beautiful old hand-hewn beams, vintage 1850s. The owner agreed to $100 for the barn, and we would clean up the site before we left. *Deal!* We set out to mark each board siding of the barn,

likewise the beams, and carefully loaded the barn onto Igor.

Bean Hill Farm was about to become a real farm with a real barn at the top of the hill. Instead of dumping the load on the ground, we unloaded it by hand, carefully separating the wood by its given numbers

Here comes another old barn for Bean Hill Farm — hauled in by Pete's tractor!

we had written on each piece. We planted four very large locust posts in the ground as the basic foundation to support the structure, the very definition of a "pole barn"; it's a non-taxable structure.

If you laid a plank over the electric fence you could drive over it, take the plank away and the fence would pop back up. I backed Igor up over our electric fence that kept in the sheep and Starfire, our goat. Pete laid the plans out on the ground and we started erecting our new barn. We hadn't gotten too far when Pete asked, "What did you do with the plans?"

"On the ground over by Igor," I said. We looked everywhere. No plans. Wait! Where is Starfire? We found him by the house still munching on the last of the papers we intended to follow to reconstruct our barn. They were gone. Starfire had eaten them for lunch. We would have to improvise. And we did just that!

By the end of the day we had the beams in place and the two-story structure stood handsomely, without its siding. "Move the truck off the fence," I yelled to Pete. "We'll secure the pen for the night to keep the sheep in." "Where are the keys?" Pete yelled across to me.

"In the truck!" I shouted.

"Nope, not here," Pete said. "Starfire was in the truck today, do you think he took them?"

"That goat will eat anything," I said.

It took two days to get the keys out of Starfire. We had to confine him to a small pen and just wait. Meanwhile, we had to rope off the truck to keep the sheep from roaming the countryside as Igor was too heavy to move off the collapsible electric fence she was sitting on.

Economics has a lot to do with even a gentlemen's farm. Taxes are assessed by the acre, but not evenly. Our house and five acres were assessed normally. The remainder of the land could be assessed at a lower rate per acre if it is farmed. To get that discount, however, you must report on your tax return an income solely from that property of a minimum of $10,000. OK, do the math. 3,000 bales of hay at $1.50 per bale = $4,500. That would leave you $5,500 short of your $10,000 goal. *What to do?*

Young Holstein heifer at Bean Hill Farm

Enter the heifers. Buying a three-day-old Holstein heifer for $25 (which we did), rearing this heifer to the age of eighteen months (which we did), artificially inseminating her (which we did), and selling her at $1,500 (which we did). Less than ten heifers a year would put you over the ten thousand dollar mark, thus helping you become a certified tax deductible gentleman farmer (which we were)!

Feeding ten heifers or more for eighteen months can be prohibitively expensive unless you produce your own feed. Again, back to the numbers. Five acres of planted corn will produce six tons of corn. Sell half the corn off and the remainder can be ground and bagged with oats and molasses to feed your heifers. Here's the good part: at the bottom of our hill is an Agway store that just so happens to grind and bag corn. So this is where we stand. We bale our own hay, grow our own corn, and feed all our animals off the land. I haven't mentioned "Big Red." It has become routine for people to ask us to retire their pets. After all, we have all this land. Before we knew it, we were feeding three horses, two cows, ten to fifteen Holstein heifers, one goat...*oops,* three goats and a few sheep. We won't count the guinea hens, chickens and pheasant.

Barn at Bean Hill Farm

Our heifers were a bit like children — they didn't enjoy seeing Dr. Murphy arrive to give them shots. Moreover, the heifers didn't appreciate getting inseminated at eighteen months. Catching a young heifer was tricky and took every ounce of a young, twenty-three-year-old veterinarian — plus myself and two additional adults to corral and hold her against the wall to be serviced. Our now pregnant heifers were ready to ship to foreign lands.

A local farmer would arrive with a cattle trailer and take them to Stewart Airport in Newburgh, NY where they were loaded onto an airplane and flown to farms all over the globe, including Brazil, Egypt, and South Africa. Once they reached their new home, they would drop a calf and go straight to the milk line. We were paid $1,400 per calf. That just about covered the cost of feeding her and covering the vet bills. Obviously, this was a labor of love that actually did cover the cost of being a gentleman farmer.

Jennifer and I thought it would be a great Christmas present for her mother to purchase two pregnant Alpine goats. We scurried off one afternoon in the old Jeep. I remember it was nearly Christmas, snow was on the ground and the temperature went up to produce a solid fog across our county. It took forever to slowly drive through the fog and back home again with the soon to be Nannies!

We backed up to the porch deck in front of the house and Jennifer ran in to get mother. "Close your eyes!" Jennifer instructed. Jean stepped on the deck, opened her eyes and there they were, two very pregnant goats almost smiling at her from the back of the Jeep.

"Merry Christmas!" we both sang out. A gift that lasts and lasts, for Jennifer anyway. She ended up with the chore of milking them daily. And she became quite proficient at the job. *Farm life!*

Settling in to Bean Hollow

"Guess what I did today?"

"You bought the Brooklyn Bridge!" was my friendly reply.

"No, silly! I did see a house though, in Clinton Corners, that you should see. The property is drop dead gorgeous, with about five acres and filled with eighty-foot pine trees all the way up the drive. It's charming." I felt it necessary to pay special attention as her speech sped up in her excitement.

"I called the real estate broker and we can see it tomorrow. The price is great as an investment and you can rebuild the house. Darling, it's a moneymaker. With our talent we can have fun, flip this place, and make a few dollars. Want to see it?" She finally paused long enough to take a breath.

She was right. The trees lining the drive were eighty feet tall and the grounds had a lot of potential. The house itself was a disaster. Walking in the front door, I discovered the room of 15' x 20' was an original chicken coop. Four additions were added to the structure pushing out on three sides. A roof was installed over the entire building leaving the old roof on the chicken coop.

Could we make this into a charming, irresistible abode? You bet. With Jean's design talent, my building ability and with our combined passion to generate a 180% can-do attitude, we decided to make an offer.

The closing went swiftly and before we knew it we were fully engaged in our new Bean Hollow project. We figured three to four months and the house would be ready to flip. Now, where to start?

Gutting the inside and stripping the asphalt brick shingles off the exterior would show us the bones of the structure and ultimately show us what needed to be done. Although the house was tiny (1,100 square feet) we found the house was not all there. The floor joists were rotted, the roof needed replacing as would all the windows and doors. The heating system and all the plumbing and electric would have to be updated. Our local construction buddies offered to bring a bulldozer over and help us get rid of this "piece of crap," as they called it, and help us to build a real house. Jean wasn't having any of it and I was right behind her.

The house developed into a perfect gem. It took a little longer than planned to complete. By the time we were halfway into the reno-vation, we knew we had a perfect home for two people. Again, that proverbial light bulb went on. *Ta–da!* That couple should be *us.*

Our Bean Hollow five-acre plot has become a playground for young and old. Jean and I have seating areas we visit to enjoy the calm. "Fern Gully" winds a path through the forest up to the stream that borders the east end of Bean Hollow. Rocks and boulders line the stream and, over the years, the grandchildren have spent hours damming the stream to create a shallow swimming hole.

Nanny and Papa have sat on the banks and enjoyed the funny, insane energy coming from half-frozen kids having the time of their little lives. The magic forest is majestic — with its giant pines ever searching for more room in the sky above.

The various areas of the property have been named by our grandchildren, Bryce, Connor, Jake and Madison. During visits to their doting Papa and Nanny, we would hook up the wagon to the old Wheel Horse tractor, fill the wagon with pillows, load the kids, and drive through the maze of secret places, stopping on occasion to tell spooky stories.

Connor, Madison, Papa, and Jake

To paraphrase an old saying, our greatest treasure in having grandchil-dren is that we don't have to raise them, we simply get to enjoy them.

On the way to Fern Gully

Jeanie Bean & Family

THE BUILDING THAT HOUSED our Clinton Corners Country Store and our Deli over a period of thirty straight years till 2010 was now intermittently occupied by other food establishments. For us, the space served as a magical place that the community enjoyed for three decades, supporting our family along the way. The store is still in its original state from 1908, with its old world charm.

Meanwhile, Jean and I had an unusual hiatus from the store; and, of course, we kept busy working on our other projects. This allowed Jean and me to keep busy working on our Lake George property, two hours north of Clinton Corners.

In 2015, our current tenant in the store gave us notice, ending their lease. We needed to find a new tenant.

During this time, Jennifer had established a wonderful baking business out of her house. Having an empty store prompted a family meeting at the old store. Jennifer's business was rapidly growing; moving into the store would solve her growing pains, not to mention resolving our new tenant search. Jeanie Bean and Company was a name of recognition and with great fanfare we decided to make a slight change calling Jennifer's new business Jeanie Bean & Family.

A trip to the lawyer and Jeanie Bean & Family was born. Mom and Dad agreed to help Jennifer create her business into a Deli/Café with a menu of fresh homemade everything. The Wow factor comes into play here and Jennifer didn't let anyone down. From her early morning breakfast creations to her lunch specials, there wasn't a dish she didn't knock out of the park. And her husband and children pitched in to add a wonderful dimension to her efforts.

Our friend Betty Martin made Irish soda bread that was out of this world. And Betty gave her recipe to Jean. Jean passed it down to Jennifer. Jennifer made the bread and went on to win first place at the

Dutchess County Fair, and then won a blue ribbon at the New York State Fair in Syracuse. One recent St. Patrick's Day week, she baked over 700 loaves of her Irish soda bread. Talented gal!

Words can't describe the success of Jennifer's new business. Her passion exceeded the 180 Rule and the community was thrilled to have the store reinvented by our family. The store seats 45 customers and the atmosphere is electric. Thanks to the internet, traffic off the Taconic has boosted sales and once new customers have found her, they return.

Walking into Jeanie Bean & Family is a trip on its own. Immediately, you are greeted by a staff that truly wants to be there. The atmosphere is quaint, homey, fun and friendly. All those things wrapped in a single experience, topping it off with Jennifer's culinary talent. My daughter is an experience in theatre. (*I wonder where she got that?*) It's a blessing to see how she has developed into a personality worthy of an Oscar. Her mother had everything to do with her ability in the kitchen, going all the way back to baking with her when she was in school. We worked hard to give Jennifer a strong work ethic and *joie de vivre,* and, brother, did she run with it. The proverbial 180 Rule!

I began helping Jennifer on the counter and as a short order cook, and Jean was in the kitchen creating the most delicious salads. Her chicken curry salad sells out daily as do her frozen dinners. Getting through the 2020 Covid 19 pandemic required a paradigm shift. Jennifer lost half her traffic to the virus. However, the New York City weekenders began to stay up in the country which prompted a run on the frozen dinners Jean was preparing. Half the people were coming in, but they were buying twice as much out of the freezer.

Our plan was to work with Jennifer for three months until she had everything under control; then we could step away and let her sail. *Three months turned into six years!* I come in twice a week and do Jennifer's books, while Jeanie Bean is still putting in the hours in the kitchen and entertaining on the floor with the customers. It's Show Time, and a whole lot of fun. Just to sit in the back room and listen to the laughter and the sound of joy coming from the staff and customers, fills the soul.

LIFE IN THE KITCHEN
We're still here...helping Jennifer
in her seventh year.

THE ACCIDENT

I'M WHAT YOU CALL AN EARLY BIRD. When my feet hit the floor, I tap dance. It's not a challenge but more like, *I just can't wait to start the day.* I'm good with three hours sleep, or nine. With only three hours, I usually nap during the day.

When Jennifer established her wonderful business in 2015 in our old Clinton Corners building, she inherited my early morning gift. Up at four, in the store by five. For the first two years she was in business, I often joined her or even opened for her. I make a delicious breakfast sandwich: apple-smoked bacon, double egg and cheese on a fresh hard roll.

It was a Tuesday morning and I left the house at 6 a.m., knowing that Jennifer had opened earlier. At my age, it was a gift to jump into my brand new Toyota Tacoma pickup truck and head out to help my darling daughter. At this point in her well-established business, I'm not sure my appearance was necessary, but I like to think it was. I was 78 years old, and 'twas a bit of a fantasy to think I still needed a pickup truck. But my wife often encourages me and says it keeps me young at heart. My black beauty slithered quietly out our tree-lined drive and on to the road heading for Clinton Corners. Eight-tenths of a mile down our Clinton Hollow Road, my life changed.

At forty miles an hour, I rounded a bend in the road to suddenly meet another pickup truck in my lane going very, very fast. That split second, I remember only the scream that came from my lungs, *"No — no!"* and my world was enveloped in brilliant white light, with an enormous pitch black circle in the center. I remember thinking *I'm somewhere surreal, out of this realm.* Then, silence.

I was pushed halfway across the passenger seat and the seatbelt was pinning me down. I couldn't move. As my eyes came into focus, I realized the cab was full of smoke and my immediate thought was *fire*. My left hand was free and to my surprise, I managed to open the driver-side door about a foot. I could feel the fresh air. I couldn't move; so I just sat there trying to control my breath.

A woman's voice came through my slightly open door, "Are you all right?" I heard her ask! "Can I call someone for you?" *What?* I couldn't believe she asked me that question. "If you could remember the number of 911 that might be helpful."

Her question was born out of anxiety — and probably helped me to relax. A strange time for levity. What I didn't know at the time was that she had already called 911 and help was on the way. The siren went off and within seconds one of our local firemen phoned Jennifer at the Deli and she too was on her way.

Matt Lawlor, of our local Matt's Auto Body in Salt Point, was the first person I recognized and actually talked with. His shop was at the end of the road. The next face I saw was Jennifer's and I assured her I was alright. I wasn't, but having her there was comforting. I couldn't stop myself from thinking *I'm gone. I'm in a dream and it didn't hurt.*

I couldn't feel anything, until I tried to move. Then it hurt like hell. *I must not be dead.*

The smoke in the cab that put me into panic mode was actually talcum powder from all the air-bags. Six of them went off and saved my life. The brilliant white light I experienced at impact was the airbag hitting my face. It was all surreal, but all made sense to me days later. The young girl responsible for the accident was seriously hurt and the triage was taking care of "her first."

It took nearly an hour before I was extracted from my truck. Don Estes, our East Clinton Fire Chief, was my extractor and savior — with words and deeds — getting me onto a backboard and into the ambulance. Assisted by fireman Ryan Figliozzi, they never left my side, keeping me safe and calm for that critical hour before I headed off in the ambulance. Jean and Jennifer followed me in their car to the hospital.

At the moment of the accident, my left hand was pushed behind the steering wheel, hitting the turn indicator, peeling the skin from the back of my hand and arm. I mention this because my left hand was resting on my left leg all during the wait for the extraction. My left leg became soaked in blood from my arm—something Don and the paramedics didn't know. They proceeded to cut my pants off, thinking my leg was injured. At the hospital, I mentioned to Jean that Don had cut my pants off. Her immediate response: "Oh dear . . . It wasn't your good linen pants, I hope!" Laughter is the best medicine.

The accident changed my life. My right arm was pushed through my back, breaking my shoulder, requiring surgery. I went through more than a year of brutal rehabilitation. My physical therapist could (and did) hurt me; yet I walked out of each session feeling better. My right foot was crushed — and rebuilding my foot came with no guarantees.

"If we can't establish an adequate blood flow after replacing the bone and reattaching your toes, we'll just have to lop it off at the ankle." Hearing those foreboding words from the surgeon, I calmly asked, "Doc, have you ever seen a one-legged tap dancer?" I didn't return.

The foot bones have calcified, so I do have pain if I step on a rock. And my foot does indeed resemble that of a duck's. But, should the Olympic Committee ever create a new aquatic sports event, I might just set a new world record for swimming in circles.

~ 15 ~

Steven Spielberg's West Side Story

WHAT A DIFFERENCE A DAY MAKES

AS FATE WOULD HAVE IT, a friendly chap visited our Clinton Corners deli in the summer of 2018. He asked my daughter Jennifer about a portrait hanging in the store. Jennifer explained that it was a portrait of her dad painted in London in 1959 while he was performing in the musical *West Side Story.*

"He's in the back," Jennifer added. "Would you like to meet him?"

Soon enough, Andrew Hoffer and I were seated at a table in the deli, having a lively conversation — with Andrew focused mainly on my 30-year career in the theatre. He seemed genuinely fascinated.

As my family will tell you, I love meeting people, chatting and telling stories. (This is the part of theatre that has never left me.)

When our congenial afternoon conversation drew to a close, Andrew Hoffer and I shook hands, thanking one another for the pleasure of our company. Since he lived in New York City, I really didn't expect to ever hear from him again.

Fast forward to nearly a year later, in the spring of 2019. We found in our email an astonishing message forwarded by Andrew Hoffer. He had written it originally to Steven Spielberg's production company, Amblin Partners; and the message would ultimately get the attention of Steven Spielberg himself.

Subject: David Bean – West Side Story
To: Amblin Partners

Understanding that you'll be starting production this summer on West Side Story, I wanted to let you know about David Bean, who played one of the Jets in the 1961 film, and was the newspaper-clutching Officer Krupke in the song "Gee, Officer Krupke."

Driving upstate from our home in Brooklyn, I pulled into a small town about 90 miles north called Clinton Corners, for

lunch at a small restaurant called Jeanie Bean & Family. Noticing a painting of a young man on the wall, I asked the woman behind the counter who he was. As it turned out, the woman was his daughter and she said. "That's my dad," and proceeded to tell me about his role in the film. To my surprise, she called for him and he came to the counter.

Painting by Patrick Larkin

Recounting several stories about making the original film, he couldn't have been more charming and engaging. His memories obviously brought him incredible joy.

I'm writing to ask if you would consider casting him in a bit part in your upcoming film. It would not only be an honor, surprise and joy for David, but might also be a sprinkle of proverbial pixie dust on your production!

Many thanks for your consideration,

Andrew Hoffer

Sometimes things simply leave you dumbfounded. What a selfless act for Andrew to put himself out and do such a thing — with results that are one in a million. I was contacted by the agency casting *West Side Story* for Amblin Partners — and another adventure began.

Up to Harlem

IT WAS SATURDAY MORNING in New York City and my pick up call was for eight o'clock at The Empire Hotel. My driver was prompt and we had a chatty drive up to Harlem.

As we pulled onto 128th Street, I was astounded at the presence of all the production trailers and equipment vans lining both sides of 130th and 131st Streets. I had initially been emailed to report to the "honey wagons," only to find out later that someone was pulling my leg. The honey wagons were the seven-stall porta-potties that appeared on the scene — resplendent in shiny aluminum, custom-built on the beds of fancy eighteen-wheelers. Very posh — and clearly attractive enough to make you want to pee just to climb aboard.

My first stop was wardrobe — another sixty-foot custom trailer built as a wardrobe department on wheels, large enough to outfit an episode of *Game of Thrones*. My arrival had been anticipated by a phone call two weeks earlier to get my measurements. This saved me a trip to Steiner Studios Costume Shop in Brooklyn. The custom-fit outfit was all ready for me.

In my role as a fabric shop owner in the '50s, I would be wearing a black pair of Baroque shoes, black trousers with suspenders, a long-sleeved white dress shirt with tiny stripes, and a vest complete with buttons, leaving the bottom one open. A tie, tie clip, and gold pocket watch completed my outfit as the fabric shop owner.

Everything fit to a T—with a fitting session that took less than a half hour. But it was the stream of questions about being in the 1961 release of *West Side Story* that ran the costume call into two hours.

OLD TIGER MEETS NEW TIGER

BACK IN MY DRESSING ROOM, I hung up my costume and was wondering how I might fill the rest of my day. It was only 11 o'clock and I wouldn't be needed for filming till early tomorrow morning.

When I stepped out of my air-conditioned dressing room trailer, I was hit by a New York City blast of summer heat. A production assistant was right there to escort me to 128th Street where Steven Spielberg was shooting a segment of the *Prologue* — with the Jets dancing in the street. I was led into a tent with several Hollywood-style chairs featuring "WEST SIDE STORY" imprinted on the back canvas strap.

There were several monitors set up showing all of the camera positions and a perfect view of the dancers as seen through the camera lens. But there was no sound. No music could be heard in the street, yet the kids were perfectly in sync and the dancing was wonderful. In our day, we had a loud speaker in the street belting out the music as we danced.

Fast forward 60 years and all the dancers now had a tiny remote ear plug that played the music; and unless you had an earplug, you couldn't hear the music at all.

The clapper could be heard for each take as the action was taking place just outside our tent. The screen burst into action without sound and the Jets filled the screen with excitement. It was at this moment that I realized these kids really did have the talent to show you they were in charge. Justin Peck's choreography was strong — danced with flair and precision necessary to maintain a don't-mess-with-me attitude. Watching the monitor without the music left no doubt in my mind that the dancing was brilliant and powerful; Peck's choreography told you that these guys did in fact own the street. (In 2014, Justin Peck had been appointed resident choreographer of the New York City Ballet, only the second person to hold that title.)

The dance shoot was over and I wandered out onto the street where the action had just taken place. Soon enough, several of the dancers were introduced to me. In fact, I became surrounded by the Jets — and hammered with questions. The air was filled with excitement and genuine interest.

I know I was caught up in the excitement, but to have these dancers react to an old Jet was mind-blowing. They all knew who I was and the questions just kept on coming.

"What was it like to work with Robbins?"

"Was he as tough as they say he was?"

Bursting through the middle of the crowd, Steven Spielberg grabbed my hand and said, "You're David Bean. *Tiger!* Well, we'll have to call you the *Old Tiger,* as we have a new one here," introducing me to Julian Elia, the *New Tiger.*

Spielberg's words were flowing out like a water fountain.

"You were in *Peter Pan* on Broadway, with Mary Martin!"

Without taking a breath he asked, "Did you know Cyril Ritchard? I did a film, *Hook,* and fashioned Hook's character after Cyril Ritchard and Terry Thomas. Hook, in my mind was a combination of both personalities. I loved that man, Cyril, he was the perfect Hook."

Old Tiger meets New Tiger: David Bean and Julian Elia

219

Relating a few stories about Cyril, I mentioned that I was writing my memoirs, which included some memorable moments on stage and screen and travel with Cyril—during a 33-year span as his surrogate son.

A voice from the crowd called out and Steven was hurried off in a flash. Justin Peck was standing to my left and introduced himself.

"Hi, I'm Justin, the choreographer. Did you get a chance to view the shoot?"

There was no hesitation in my reply, as I told him of my initial fear that the dancing here would be beautiful, but lack an inner strength that one would associate with a New York City gang — something that Jerome Robbins would have gone to extraordinary lengths to create.

"Well, all I can say now," I said, "is that if the remainder of your work is as strong and believable as I saw twenty minutes ago, then you'll knock it out of the park!"

After watching only sixteen bars of the *Prologue*, it was abundantly clear to me that Justin Peck had indeed nailed it.

Steven reappeared still full of energy, making you feel as if you were the most important person on the planet. He was so approachable and such a good listener.

We stood there in the middle of 128th Street, in the maze of cameras, mic booms, sun screens and film crews, talking excitedly and loudly to be heard over the constant noise in the street. Every word we exchanged was being recorded for a documentary of the making of *West Side Story*.

Perched next to a nearby camera was Laurent Bouzereau, a behind-the-scenes documentary filmmaker, capturing our conversation. As we talked, he would interject with "Repeat that question" and "Old Tiger, tell us about how it feels to be back on the street with the Jets!"

I couldn't help but feel like a rock star. Imagine. All these dancers growing up watching the 1961 film version of *West Side Story* and having our movie influence them to become dancers. To top it off, they were genuinely excited to tell me about it.

I was blindsided by the attention of each and every Jet telling me his story and just what the original film meant to him and my being there to share the moment. I wasn't prepared for this. Whenever I recount that entire afternoon, I become very emotional.

THE SHOOT

A T 6 A.M. SHARP, my driver arrived and we made our way to Harlem. Again, the caravan of trailers and equipment trucks lined the streets. My dressing room had "CAST MEMBER 85" taped on the door. A script and a contract were on a side table, near my costume, which was neatly hanging on a rack. Included in my wardrobe was a cotton undershirt to absorb the anticipated perspiration. The temperature outside was on its way up from the early morning 70s, expected to level out in the 80s.

Dressed as a fabric store owner, I met my escort at the door and we made my our way to the makeup trailer. It was good to be accompanied by someone who knew the territory (comforting for one who could easily get lost in the maze of a street jammed with equipment). It was an impressive makeup department on eighteen wheels. In makeup, my hair was the issue. You see, my hair has a curl and I wear it straight up like a curly crewcut. I hadn't been in the chair two minutes when I felt something like pomade being massaged into my hair. By the time I looked up to see the hairdresser's progress, my jaw dropped.

"You parted my hair!" I exclaimed.

"Yes," she said, "I think it looks appropriate, sort of early '50s period."

I was in mild shock.

"The last time my hair was parted was in 1947!" I said, knowing full well that I would lose the battle to look like a youngish fabric store owner.

Before the rehearsal for the shoot began, Steven Spielberg took me aside and explained that in the 1950s the white store owners upped the prices when the Puerto Ricans purchased their items. Naturally, this policy upset them. It was commonplace in those days.

Our first rehearsal started. On the set were the Shark boys (including *Bernardo,* played by David Alvarez) and *Anita* (played by Ariana De-Bose). As the Sharks came nearer, *Anita* started to sing. She, of course, had the remote earplug and could hear the music. I, on the other hand, couldn't hear a thing, so when she belted out, "Buying on credit is so nice," I jumped, not expecting it. We rehearsed that bit several times, and each time I had to guess when something was about to happen. Giving *Bernardo* a dirty look wasn't difficult. After all, he gave it to me first. I just gave it back, and then they would leave, going down the street from me.

Anita practiced the passing of the credit slip she was to sign, as well as taking the package from my sales girl, as *Bernardo* would snatch the credit slip from *Anita*'s hand. After several rehearsals, Steven called for a take. The next thing I heard was the clapper to coordinate the sound. We were ready to roll!

From the corner of my eye, I followed the camera up the street to where *Anita* and I were standing and, at the right time, I handed the pen and paper to *Anita* for her signature. As planned, *Bernardo* took the receipt and gave me a dirty look while singing, "One look at us and they charge twice!" I gave him the expected dirty look back, and they moved down the street. *"Cut"* could be heard from a distance and we all relaxed.

A few minutes later, Steven appeared and said, "It was perfect. We don't need another. Very good everyone, well done. That's a wrap!"

That, my friends, is what is called a cameo roll. Ten to fifteen seconds at best — and it came with direction.

Within seconds, the crew was breaking down the set to move down two blocks to set up again, continuing the long process of getting a major film in the can.

As I was stepping off the set, Steven walked over to me and reminded me to send him my manuscript. He said he would love to read it. I thanked him, we shook hands, and I scooted off to wardrobe to change back into my street clothes.

My driver picked me up and dropped me off at Grand Central Station for the beautiful two-hour train ride north to Clinton Corners, thus ending a more than spectacular weekend for *Old* Tiger.

$\mathbb{E}$*pilogue*

ANOTHER TWENTY YEARS

$\mathbb{A}$S JEAN AND I APPROACH our 60th wedding anniversary, we've been speculating lately about the passing of time and the speed with which it travels. We seriously ask ourselves, "What's next?" As you've read, our lives have come full circle. Our first encounter with *West Side Story* was 62 years ago, and our connection continues to the present. To sit down now and take life easy is not in our DNA. With 26 career changes under our belt, what we get involved with next isn't as important as mustering the passion to do it.

We will always be there for our family and friends, especially our daughter Jennifer with her venture at Jeanie Bean & Family. To mingle amongst the familiar local faces that have accompanied and supported our family these past forty years is life-giving. They have truly become part of our family. We're grateful for the "other half" of the dance that makes it come alive.

Should you ever find yourself in Dutchess County, you must pop in and treat yourself to the slice of magic we experience daily. Savor the atmosphere and enjoy a taste of our extraordinary, ordinary way of life.

Always remembering,
"When you're a Jet you're a Jet all the way."

The dance continues . . .

Acknowledgments

THERE IS AN AMAZING TEAM OF PEOPLE who went to work putting this book together. If it weren't for their 180% efforts and encouragement, this book would never have been.

First on my list is Mrs. Bean, my mate. Her encouragement and patience are heaven sent. Brutal at times, but necessary and loving.

Joseph "Trip" Sinnott never lost faith and put in a million hours without complaint. Jean and I have been fans of his for the past 40 years. From start to finish, Trip is the man you want to be in the room with. As a publisher and collaborator, he's fun and knowledgeable, with an eye like a hawk. We love him dearly.

My life in the theatre and dance has been unbelievably fortunate — being directed and tutored by some of the best talent of our time. Now, my first attempt at putting a book together has introduced me to a new world of talent for whom I wholeheartedly applaud and thank.

To Maggie Adams, who unearthed gems from MGM's 1961 *West Side Story* archives, including the photo that graces our front cover, which she described as a "rare, never-before-seen photograph." It was a great treat to work with Maggie and the team at MGM, including Ben Houston and Clayton Henry.

To Jessica and Frank Mazzella at Printing and Graphic Concepts who outdid themselves with the 180% rule all along the way.

With great gratitude to Tim and Yvonne Walsh for their amazing dedication to the project — from early 2020 right through the pre-press homestretch and beyond.

To Katie Olson at KnockOut, Inc. in Minnesota for her invaluable roles as print manager, eagle-eyed reviewer, and super-timely responder—joined in her book review collaboration by *West Side Story* aficionado Pete Klatt.

There are countless members of our team who contributed with equal enthusiasm from the wings. For taking this extraordinary journey with me, my heartfelt thanks go to: Michael Korda, Lee Kravitz, Andrew Hoffer, Leigh Knickerbocker, Diane and Vince Sauter, Mark Farmer, Phillippa Ewing Weiland, Ted Schluenderfritz, Tom and Julie Currie, Kathleen Corby, Luke and Abby Angell, and Paul Schaefer.

To all our friends at Jeanie Bean & Family Deli & Café who have shared and enhanced our lives in Clinton Corners, creating a lifetime of wonderful memories and stories over the past 40 years. *Thanks, mates!*

To Brittani Lindman, the rock of Amblin Partners. Thank you for all your sincere interest and time spent on our behalf. You are a treasure.

Finally, my gratitude goes to Steven Spielberg, for giving me a timely ending to this book—with the special privilege of playing a tiny part in your 2021 production of *West Side Story*.

Illustration Credits

With thankfulness to all those who so kindly collaborated with us in enhancing the book with gems from their collections, we offer these credits, comments, and copyright notices:

Cover Photographs:

Front Cover: **David Bean in the *Prologue****

Note: When she brought this 60-year-old gem to the table for our consideration, MGM's Maggie Adams realized, "In my 33 years in the photo archives at MGM, I'd never seen it, nor was it ever used in any of our design work." *Thank you, Maggie, for unearthing our cover photo!*

Back cover: **Jets singing the *Jet Song****

Spine: **David "Tiger" Bean****

* West Side Story © 1961 Metro-Goldwyn-Mayer Studios Inc.
All Rights Reserved • Courtesy of MGM Media Licensing.

Front Matter and
Chapter 1: *Growing Up a Bean*

First page: Silhouette drawing of David Bean by Ted Schluenderfritz. *Note:* All of the small silhouette drawings of David "Tiger" Bean throughout the book are original illustrations by Ted Schluenderfritz, Littleton, CO.

Dedication page: Photo of David, Jeanie and Jennifer at Bean Hollow by Jubilee Studio 33, Clinton Corners, NY.

Page 6: David Bean in *West Side Story,* London production, 1958: Photographer: Angus McBean. *Courtesy of the author, from the Bean family's personal collection of photo albums and scrapbooks.*

Pages 13, 16, 17, 18: The Bean family photos on these four pages are *courtesy of the author, from the Bean family's personal collection.*

Chapter 2: *Peter Pan*

Pages 20, 21 and 26: 1954 publicity photos from *Peter Pan, preserved in the Bean family's personal collection of photo albums and scrapbooks.*

Page 29: "Curtain up at Sardi's": November 1954 birthday party photo, *preserved in the Bean family's personal collection.* Featuring the thirteen celebrants at 13-year-old Heller Halliday's birthday party:

BIRTHDAY GUESTS AT SARDI'S *(see page 29, left to right)*
Bucko Stafford, Robert Harrington, Alan Sutherland,
Jackie Scholle, Arthur Pollick, Ronnie Lee, Heller Halliday,
Margalo Gillmore, Vincent Sardi, David Bean,
Stan Stenner, Linda Dangcil, Darryl Duran.

Pages 31, 32, 36: 1954 publicity photos from *Peter Pan, preserved in the Bean family's personal collection.*

Page 33: Madge Elliott and Cyril Ritchard, dancing partners. *Courtesy of the author.*

Page 34: Cyril and Madge's Wedding, Australia 1935: *Courtesy of the State Library of New South Wales.*

Page 36: Mary Martin and the Lost Boys: *Courtesy of the author, from the Bean family's personal collection of photo albums and scrapbooks.*

Chapter 3: *Interlude*

Pages 37, 38, 39, 49: Photos: *Courtesy of the author, from the Bean family's personal collection of photo albums and scrapbooks.*

Page 47: 1956 postcard of the Royal Hawaiian Hotel: *Courtesy of Jubilee Studio 33, Clinton Corners, NY.*

Chapter 4: *West Side Story* (London Production)

Page 51: Portion of *West Side Story* 1961 movie poster: *Courtesy of MGM Media Licensing • West Side Story © 1961 Metro-Goldwyn-Mayer Studios Inc. All Rights Reserved.*

Pages 58-59: Portions of the 1958 Pan Am booklet presented to those aboard the lavish *West Side Story* flight from NY to England, November 7, 1958. *Courtesy of the author, from the Bean family's personal collection of photo albums and scrapbooks.*

Page 56: West Side Story "Cool" Rehearsals at the Alvin Theater, NYC. *Preserved in the Bean family's personal collection of photo albums.*

Page 61: Sketch of Her Majesty's Theatre by Jean Webber *Courtesy of the author, from the Bean family's personal collection of photo albums and scrapbooks.*

Page 62: David and Jerry Robbins, Opening Night in London, 1958. *Courtesy of the author, from the Bean family's personal collection of photo albums and scrapbooks.*

Page 65: George Chakiris and David Bean biking at Eccleston Mews in London. *Courtesy of the author, from the Bean family's personal collection of photo albums and scrapbooks.*

Page 66: Portrait of David Bean. Photographer: Jeremy Grayson. *Courtesy of the author, from the Bean family's personal collection of photo albums and scrapbooks.*

Pages 68, 70, 72, 73, 77, 78, 84, 85: Photos, portraits, and paintings. *Courtesy of the author, from the Bean family's personal collection of photo albums and scrapbooks.*

Page 71: Princess Margaret greeting cast members. *By permission and license from Keystone Press / Alamy Stock Photo.*

Page 75: Photo taken during *West Side Story's* London production by Angus McBean. *Courtesy of Harvard University, Houghton Library.*

Chapter 5: *Enter Miss Jean Deeks*

Pages 86, 89, 92: London photos of Jean Deeks and family. *Preserved in the Bean family's personal collection of photo albums.*

Chapter 6: *West Side Story* (1961 Movie)

With special thanks to Maggie, Ben and Clayton at MGM, we gratefully acknowledge that Chapter 6, focusing on the 1961 movie *West Side Story,* has been greatly enhanced by the inclusion of still photos and screen shots from the archives of MGM, featured on:

Pages 94, 97, 98, 100, 101, 107, 108, 109, 111, 114.

West Side Story © 1961 Metro-Goldwyn-Mayer Studios Inc. All Rights Reserved • Courtesy of MGM Media Licensing.

Additional illustrations in Chapter 6:

Page 105: Photo of Natalie Wood *(Maria)* on the set of the 1961 *West Side Story* movie, courtesy of the author. Photographer: David Bean.
Page 110: Photo of George Chakiris. Photographer: Angus McBean. *Courtesy of the author, from the Bean family's personal collection of photo albums and scrapbooks.*
Page 113: Publicity photo of Jerome Robbins: in the public domain.
Page 115: 2011 photograph of four cast members of the 1961 film. *Courtesy of the author, from the Bean family's personal collection of photo albums and scrapbooks.*

Chapter 7: *West Side Story (British Tour)*

Page 116, 118, 122, 123: Photos and Leeds Grand Theatre poster. *Courtesy of the author, from the Bean family's personal collection of photo albums and scrapbooks.*
Page 120: Photo: "After the Rumble," with David Holliday *(Tony)* and Jean Deeks *(Anybodys)*. Photographer: Angus McBean. *Courtesy of Harvard University, Houghton Library.*

Chapter 8: *Our Wedding*

Pages 126, 129, 130: 1962 Wedding Photos of David and Jean Bean. *Courtesy of the author, from the Bean family's personal collection of photo albums and scrapbooks.*

Chapter 9: *Return to New York*

Pages 132, 134, 137, 139: Photos and *Around the World in 80 Days* poster. *Courtesy of the author, from the Bean family's personal collection of photo albums and scrapbooks.*

Chapter 10: *Fifty Miles*

Pages 143, 145, 146: Three photos. *Courtesy of the author, from the Bean family's personal collection of photo albums and scrapbooks.*
Page 144: Printer's Ornament: "Lion: Courage." Courtesy of Mies Hora, Ultimate Symbol, Inc. © 1994 All rights reserved.
Page 149: Sketch of Shrub Oak Gallery by Don Lambo for the Beans.

Chapter 11: *Enter Jennifer*

Pages 152, 155, 156, 159, 160, 161, 162, 165, 167: Bean family photos. *Courtesy of the author, from the Bean family's personal collection of photo albums—with several photos texted to him for page 167 from the two younger generations.*

Chapter 12: *Glimpses of Life After West Side Story*

Pages 168, 173, 179, 185, 186: Photos and images. *Courtesy of the author, from the Bean family's personal collection of photo albums, scrapbooks, and songsheets.*

Chapter 13: *Cyril's Final Curtain Call*

Pages 188, 191: Two photos of Cyril Ritchard. *Courtesy of the author, from the Bean family's personal collection of photo albums.*

Chapter 14: *Moving North: Another Life*

Pages 198, 201, 203, 205, 206, 208, 211: Photos of life in Clinton Corners. *Courtesy of the author, from the Bean family's personal collection of photo albums and scrapbooks.*

Chapter 15: *Steven Spielberg's West Side Story*

Page 216: Portrait of David Bean by painter Patrick Lambert Larkin (1907–1981). This portrait currently hangs in the Jeanie Bean and Family Deli and Café. *Courtesy of the author.*

Page 219: "Old Tiger Meets New Tiger: David Bean and Julian Elia." *Photo by Niko Tavernise. © 2021 20th Century Studios. All Rights Reserved. Courtesy of Amblin Partners—with our gratitude to Brittani Lindman and Steven Spielberg for permission to use.*

Epilogue

Page 224: Photo of David and Jean Bean. *Courtesy of their daughter Jennifer.*

Last Page

Page 240: Photo of their swing. *Courtesy of David and Jean Bean.*

Index of People

For Jean, who loves this swing.
From David, who always sits beside her.